The Brera Gallery

The Brera Gallery

Electa

On the cover
Donato Bramante, Christ at the Column, detail.

Translation
David Stanton

Contents

The Brera: History
of an Art Gallery

Rosalba Tardito

When we speak of the Brera we are not only referring to a great art gallery, but also to that group of institutions, including the Academy of Fine Art, the Library, the Observatory and the Lombard Institute of Science, Letters and Arts, which carry on their various activities in a building which has played an outstanding role in the history of Milan.

As a State museum, the Brera Art Gallery had a somewhat unusual beginning, which may be linked to that of the Gallerie dell'Accademia in Venice and the Bologna Pinacoteca. But first of all it is necessary to take a look at the origins and the historical vicissitudes of the Palazzo di Brera. It seems that in 1171, on an area of grassland known as "Brayda," a building was constructed for the Humiliati, who, following a bull issued by Pope Innocent III in 1201, became a true religious order subject to monastic rules.

Their monastery with its accompanying cloister was enhanced around 1240 by the building of the church of Santa Maria. In 1347 the Pisan Giovanni di Balduccio completed the church and the decoration with the sculptures of the white marble portal. The Humiliati order was at the height of its glory from the fourteenth to the sixteenth centuries owing to its involvement in the wool industry, together with its religious and cultural activities. In fact, many frescoes embellished the church, which was partly the work of a Tuscan artist associated with Giusto dei Menabuoi; in the sacristy there were frescoes by the Lombard Vincenzo Foppa and an altarpiece by Bernadino Luini dated 1515, the *Virgin and Child with Saint Anthony Abbot and Saint Barbara*. However, the abundant wealth led to such a degree of moral laxity that in 1571 Charles Borromeo, as part of his campaign to promote greater rigour among the clergy, obtained from Pope Pius V the dissolution of the order. With a papal bull, in 1572 the monastery became the property of the Jesuits, who founded a college. Although it was not inferior to other Italian cities in any way, at that time Milan lacked both a college and a university.

Due to the importance of the subjects taught there, in a short time the Jesuit college became a university; soon there were two thousand students, consequently the need was felt to expand and modernise the building. The design of this was entrusted to the Milanese architect Martino Bassi between 1580 and 1589. The plans were entirely revised by Francesco Maria Richini (the drawings are in the Biblioteca Ambrosiana and the Biblioteca Trivulziana). The lecture halls, the library and the main stairway, which still exists, with two flights of stairs from the courtyard surrounded by loggias were built between 1600 and 1700. In 1764 an observatory with a square tower was built by the Jesuit priest Ruggero Giuseppe Boscovich; it was considered to be one of the best in Europe in the late eighteenth century.

Thanks to the reforms carried out by Empress Maria Theresa, Milan enjoyed a long period of peace and prosperity. The Jesuit order was dissolved in 1773 and Brera College became a secular institution.

Meanwhile the Academy of Fine Art was set up in 1776, so that "the arts of painting, sculpture, architecture and ornamental design might be taught free of charge by skilled teachers." The administration of the Academy was entrusted to a "permanent secretary." Also in 1774 the Botanical Garden was established. However, all these new developments required the building to be further expanded. The planning of this was entrusted in 1774 to the "Archducal and State" architect Giuseppe Piermarini. He enlarged the library, creating the Sala Teresiana (still extant); from the former monastery he obtained the rooms for the Academy, taking as his model the one in Vienna which had been designed by Jadot. In 1775 he expanded the Observatory, in which new instruments were fitted, and improved the Botanical Garden with the building of a number of hothouses. The magnificent portal in the centre of the recently completed façade was also the work of Piermarini. Thus in this building were gathered not only the schools which had been transferred from religious administration to direct State control, but also the new institutions, to which should be added the Società Patriottica (Patriotic Society), which later became the Institute of Science, Letters and Arts. In 1778 Abbot Bianconi was appointed secretary of the Academy. Of Bolognese extraction, he was an erudite scholar and collector of drawings; for the benefit of the students' education he decided to expand the collection of prints, drawings and cartoons. But he did not encourage the collection of paintings as he was "not much interested" in this field. Thus the attempt to create an art gallery around 1790 did not bear fruit. In fact, a number of paintings by Cesare da Sesto from the church of San Rocco and a *Virgin and Child* by Aurelio Luini were disposed of to the Count Melzi d'Eril. Also other paintings from monasteries which had been closed had a similar fate. Among these were works by Perugino and Bernardino Luini from the Certosa at Pavia and the *Virgin of the Rocks* by Leonardo da Vinci from San Francesco Grande in Milan.

After they had been refused by Joseph II, who considered that there were already too many paintings from these schools in Vienna, and had not been kept by the Brera Academy they were eventually sold off to private individuals. The painting by Leonardo was sold to Lord Hamilton in 1775 (it is now in the National Gallery in London) and the other works went to Count Melzi d'Eril in 1786. With the arrival of Napoleon the development of the arts and culture continued, with the linking of the past and present for "the enlightenment of the public." In 1801 Giuseppe Bossi became secretary and he was responsible in 1803 for the official opening of the Academy as a National Academy, which thus occupied all the parts of the building which had been constructed by Piermarini.

With the dissolution of the religious orders many paintings intended for different institutions arrived. One of these was the Art Gallery of the Palace of Science and Arts of Milan (this was the official title of the Palazzo di Brera at the time). Among the first to arrive were nine paintings from the suppressed church of Santi Cosma e Damiano alla Scala, among which were the *Holy Family* by Pompeo Batoni and *Saint Jerome* and the *Crucifixion* by Pierre Subleyras (now in the room where eighteenth century paintings are displayed). Between 1805 and 1806 many works having various origins were sent by the General Administration of State Property: from (for example the *Crucifixion* by Bramantino) and from various departments of the Kingdom of Italy. Andrea Appiani was appointed Commissioner for Fine Art, and he was given the task of building up the collection.

In 1806 Viceroy Hortense de Eugène de Beauharnais donated to the Academy the *Marriage of the Virgin* by Raphael (it was formerly in Città di Castello) and the *Virgin and Child* by Giovanni Bellini, dated 1510, together with other paintings. In Milan Napoleon ordered that there should be a National Museum which was to be the most prestigious in the Kingdom of Italy.

The origin of the Brera Art Gallery was exclusively due—with the exception of the small collection which was largely created by Bossi—to the despoliation and suppression of the property of the Church. It came into existence without a real past and only began to develop in the early years of the nineteenth century. Bossi resigned in 1807 after a disagreement with the Minister of the Interior Di Breme. He was succeeded by Canon Zanoja and Appiani became keeper of the newly established Brera Art Gallery.

Appiani aimed to obtain as many important works as possible, without paying attention to repetition, and he did not have any plans for a collection chosen on a rational basis. From that time onwards real responsibility lay with the minister himself. The political power was concentrated in the hands of the Viceroy Eugène de Beauharnais, who wished to develop the Brera, in other words to provide the Academy with more space and to construct a larger building for the art gallery. Hence Appiani was responsible for the destruction of the church of Santa Maria, one of the most remarkable examples of medieval architecture in Milan, in order to allow the architect, Pietro Gilardoni, to create the art gallery, as well as the splitting up of the Galleria dell'Arcivescovado (Archbishop's Gallery), founded in 1650 by Cardinal Cesare Monti "following the example of the galleries of the Roman princes," thereby giving rise to a "dispersal of works which continued until at least 1896." In this way the Napoleonic rooms were created, with the columns forming the division between each room and skylights to allow them to be illuminated from above in accordance with the canons of the Neoclassical museums.

9

A steady stream of paintings continued to arrive. In 1808 the first group arrived, consisting of frescoes removed from Milanese churches (including works by Gaudenzio Ferrari and Marco d'Oggiono from Santa Maria della Pace, Bernardino Luini from the chapel of San Francesco in the same church and Foppa and Luini from the sacristy of Santa Maria di Brera). Other new arrivals included paintings by Vittore Carpaccio, *Saint Jerome* by Titian and the *Virgin and Child* by Mantegna. The art gallery was ready to receive paintings in 1809 (even though there are doubts concerning the inauguration which has often been referred to, but which is totally lacking in documentation, in August 1809 on the occasion of the Emperor's birthday).

In 1809 the large painting by Gentile and Giovanni Bellini, *Saint Mark Preaching at Alexandria*, arrived. In 1811 no less than four hundred and sixty-seven paintings were sent to the Brera, among which were the *Finding of the Body of Saint Mark* by Tintoretto, the *Pietà* by Giovanni Bellini, the *Saint Luke Polyptych* by Mantegna and the *Madonna and Child with Federigo da Montefeltro* by Piero della Francesca. In the same year twenty-three paintings came from the Galleria dell'Arcivescovado, the Cardinal Monti bequest, mainly from the Lombard school. In 1815 there were three hundred and five paintings displayed in the gallery. However, at the same time in the inventory (published by the Soprintendenza per i Beni Artistici e Storici of Milan in 1976) there were eight hundred and ninety-two. Thus not all the works were on display; it is true that this may have been due to a deliberate choice, but it was also the result of a lack of space. The way in which the Brera collection had been built up contained the seeds of its subsequent dispersal. When Napoleon fell, the allied powers ordered that the works of art which had been taken to France should be restored to their countries of origin, even though this obligation was only partially respected. Only twenty-four paintings were returned to their original owners. Exchanges had already taken place between Paris and Milan some years earlier: in 1812 five Lombard paintings went to the Louvre and five works by foreign artists, among which was the famous *Last Supper* by Rubens, came to the Brera. During the 1850s a number of changes took place in the gallery; paintings were sent on loan to Lombard churches.

In 1855, for the first time, a group of works came to the gallery from a private collection that had a precise orientation, as it was particularly focused on painting of the Quattrocento and landscape (works by Carlo and Vittore Crivelli, views by Francesco Guardi); this was the Cavalier Pietro Oggioni bequest, containing a total of approximately eighty works.

It is curious to learn from a book about the Brera written in 1873 by Antonio Caimi, secretary of the Academy, that it was only possible to visit the gallery by special request; the staff consisted of a keeper who doubled as restorer, a caretaker and two attendants. In 1892 the Brera became a State Art Gallery and was separated from the Academy. Under the administration of Giuseppe Bertini it was opened to the public with an entrance fee which the law promulgated by Bonghi allowed to be used for the purchase of new works. If only this were still the case today! In 1895 another sixteen works from the Monti bequest entered the gallery.

The dispersal of the frescoes by Bernardino Luini in the Villa La Pelucca in Sesto San Giovanni, painted between 1521 and 1523—which went partly to private individuals and partly to foreign collections, except for nine kept in the Brera—is an eloquent demonstration of how a museum "can give a veneer of respectability to transactions which are really quite unacceptable." For exchanges which were not always worthwhile paintings by Carlo Crivelli went to Frankfurt (Städelsches Kunstinstitut), London (National Gallery) and Venice (Gallerie dell'Accademia). Most of this dispersal was due to the fact that it was not possible to keep a substantial collection of works of art because of the lack of space. The paintings were never sent back to the place they originally came from, so that it is quite surprising, for example, that important works by one of the most famous Venetian painters of the late Seicento and early Settecento were sent to small villages like Somaglia Lodigiana. Under Corrado Ricci (1898-1903) the gallery was extended by the building of eight new rooms, and the paintings were arranged on a chronological and regional basis, more or less as they are at present. Not only did he compile a catalogue (in 1907), but he also constructed storerooms, photographic archives and skylights so the works could be illuminated by daylight. In 1903 about sixty paintings were donated by Signor Casimiro Sipriot; in the same year the new gallery was opened. New paintings arrived, the gallery was rebuilt, while no less than two hundred and nine paintings and sixty-six sculptures, all by nineteenth century artists, were sent to the Galleria Civica in Milan. Carlo Ricci must also be credited with the purchase of the frescoes by Bramante from Palazzo Panigarola. Under Ettore Modigliani (1908-34) the policy of purchases and gifts continued.

After the First World War he carried out another substantial rebuilding of the gallery, commissioning the work from the architect Piero Portaluppi, who continued with this task for forty years "linking his name to the

rebirth of the Brera after two world wars."
The inauguration took place in 1925 in the
presence of King Victor Emmanuel III.

Modigliani was responsible for the displaying
of the Brera's two most famous masterpieces
in a single room, the *Marriage of the Virgin*
by Raphael and the *Madonna and Child with
Federigo da Montefeltro* by Piero della Francesca, together with the *Virgin and Child* by
Luca Signorelli.

In 1926 the Associazione degli Amici di Brera
e dei Musei Milanesi (Association of Friends
of the Brera and Milanese Museums) was set
up with the task of fostering Milan's art heritage, especially the part of it that is to be
found in the Brera. In this period various new
paintings arrived: two views of Venice by Canaletto, the *Madonna del Carmelo* by Tiepolo and *Rebecca at the Well* by Piazzetta. It
was the Amici di Brera who donated *The Pergola* by Silvestro Lega and two portraits of
Francesco Sforza and Bianca Maria Sforza attributed to Bonifacio Bembo.

In 1927 a single Superintendency was created
for both medieval and modern art. In 1937 the
Red Wagon by Fattori was purchased and in
1939 the Amici donated Caravaggio's *Supper
at Emmaus*, which was presented to the public with an exhibition in 1940.

However, besides these admirable achievements, there was the obligation to give to
public institutions, such as embassies and
ministries, works for purely decorative purposes, simply to adorn their premises. Bossi's
portrait gallery was plundered most ruth-
lessly because works of this kind were more
suitable for a decorative function than sacred
paintings. Thus the self-portrait of Bottani is
now at the headquarters of the Third Army
Corps, the Legani and Gianoli are in the offices of the Administration of the Province of
Milan and others, including a *Roman Courte-
san* by Simon Vouet are in the office of the
Attorney General of the Republic. Four landscapes by Magnasco went to the Italian Embassy in London.

Under the administration of Guglielmo Pac-
chioni (1939-1946), Ettore Modigliani (1946-

Palazzo di Brera, staircase, detail.

Palazzo di Brera, Apartment of the Astronomer with the Jesi and Jucker Collections.

71) and Fernanda Wittgens (1947-57) various important events occurred. The Second World War broke out and the paintings in the Brera were sent to various localities. In August 1945 the Palazzo di Brera was severely damaged and the rooms in the gallery were partly destroyed.

Rebuilding began in 1946 under the supervision of Portaluppi, although the work on the wing containing Rooms 7 and 9 to 14 was carried out by Franco Albini. In the same year Guido Cagnola donated the extremely famous *Virgin and Child* by Ambrogio Lorenzetti. The paintings and their frames were restored. Since 1939 they had not been seen, as they had been closed up in cases during the war. The rebuilding lasted from 1946 to 1950. The rooms were illuminated by daylight through skylights with blinds and heating was provided by radiant panels with underfloor tubes; an air of magnificence was conferred by the marble obtained from the Opificio delle Pietre Dure in Florence.

In a special room next to the Gallery of Lombard Frescoes was displayed the fourteenth century cycle of anonymous Lombard artists belonging to the school of Giovanni da Milano, formerly in the Oratory of the Porro family at Mocchirolo near Lentate, north of Milan.

Following the rebuilding the number of gifts increased: the *Resurrection* by Cariani, the *Spring Pastures* by Segantini and the *Agony in the Garden* by Francesco del Cairo are just a few of the most important ones. In 1971 three noteworthy purchases were added: the *Christ the Judge*, by Giovanni da Milano from the Contini Bonacossi collection in Florence, the forty-eight Visconti tarot cards by Bonifacio Bembo and *Saint Charles Borromeo in Glory* by Giulio Cesare Procaccini.

Unfortunately twenty-four years after the gallery was reopened thanks to the efforts of Ettore Modigliani and Fernanda Wittgens slowly but surely conditions deteriorated, largely as a result of the lack of funds for routine maintenance of the building. The reopening of the gallery, the gifts and purchases were indeed great achievements, but water started to seep into the building and a number of rooms had to be closed. In 1971 the situation steadily grew worse. In 1973 Franco Russoli succeeded Gian Alberto Dell'Acqua (1957-73). Due to lack of funds, the various problems of the gallery and the shortage of staff, in June 1974 the gallery was closed.

With the purchase in 1972 of Palazzo Citterio, formerly Rosemberg-Colorni, an attempt was made to provide for the increased space and various services which visitors today demand from a modern museum. It was to become the hub of a project that linked two buildings through the Botanical Garden, together with other buildings in order to form a "great arts complex" in the centre of Milan.

In 1976 there was an event of great importance. Maria Jesi donated most of her collection in accordance with the wishes of her husband Emilio, who had died two years previously. In it there were fifty paintings of great significance by twentieth century Italian artists, including works by various Futurists, Morandi, Modigliani, De Pisis, Sironi, Carrà and de Chirico. In the same year Riccardo and Magda Jucker loaned to the Brera about twenty works by Futurists and artists belonging to other modern movements. Thus an important collection of twentieth century art was set up in the Brera Gallery.

In 1976 and 1977 Russoli, whose premature death occurred in the latter year, staged an exhibition entitled "Processo al Museo" (The Museum on Trial). "It is not only a trial of the shortcomings of the organisation and management of museums in Italy, but it is also an attempt to provide facts and figures, results... and proposals for a radical reform of the museums."

Russoli was succeeded by Stella Matalon (1977-78) and then Carlo Bertelli (1978-84). Fortunately damage to the skylights was repaired very speedily, but in that year only two hundred works were on exhibit and they did not include the panel paintings or the very large pictures. In December 1978 most of the rooms were reopened, while in Room 38 the Jucker and Jesi collections were hung. The works in Palazzo Citterio were going ahead very slowly, so makeshift solutions were found in the Brera Gallery. A bookshop was set up in the entrance hall, a snack bar established in the loggia and two storerooms were carved out of the rooms, thereby penalizing the collection of Seicento painting in Lombardy.

The modern collection was moved to a newly-acquired apartment which had been renovated by Ignazio Gardella. A staircase designed by Studio Alberico and Ludovico Belgioioso now leads to a mezzanine floor situated between the attics and the gallery floor, where in 1978 the first part of the offices of the Soprintendenza per i Beni Artistici e Storici of Milan were installed. They were completed in 1984.

In 1985 I was responsible for the commissioning from Studio Gregotti e Associati the preparation of a feasibility study which was to consider possible technological developments, further expansion and a rational distribution of the paintings in the gallery. For some time it had been clear that the Brera Gallery was in dire need of renovation and modernisation. The skylights and blinds needed replacing since they were in a pitiful state. The panes composed of wire glass were encrusted in dirt and soot, the metal fittings corroded and often in need of repair. Consequently the following provisions were considered to be necessary: double glazing with anti-ultraviolet film to be fitted; an air conditioning plant to be installed capable of eliminating the problems regarding the paintings that have occurred in the past because of changes in temperature or humidity; the present heating system to be eliminated, as it is quite unreliable in some parts of the building. To this end contact was made with specialists in various fields, in particular with the ENEA (National Council for Nuclear and Alternative Energy) for the drawing up of a plan for a new air conditioning plant for the exhibition rooms and service areas of the gallery, and with architect Piero Castiglioni for

Palazzo di Brera, staircase.

problems connected with the lighting (it should be noted that he had already achieved excellent results in this field in collaboration with Gae Aulenti in the Centre Pompidou and Museé d'Orsay in Paris, as well as in Palazzo Grassi in Venice).

The outline plan provides for:

a) the greatest possible area of the surface of the main floor is to be made available for the display of paintings;

b) the rooms formerly occupied by the offices will be used for the display of works of the Trecento and Quattrocento, especially those on panels and with gold grounds;

c) the paintings of the Cinquecento and Seicento—especially the Lombard and Venetian ones—will be further increased in quantity and will be hung on a thematic basis;

d) all the paintings in the Brera will be displayed in a clearer and more informative manner, although for certain collections—especially those in the Napoleonic rooms—great changes are not foreseen, due to the large dimensions of the paintings at present on display.

The paintings will be hung in a traditional manner in chronological order and according to region of origin. Besides, an attempt is being made to create architectural unity between the different parts of the building, although the contrasting styles of the Napoleonic rooms, the Jesi rooms, the Albini Gallery and the Raphael room (completed in 1983) will be respected.

In the last few years there has been a considerable increase in attention to questions of cultural interest on the part of the private sector and, generally speaking, the relationship between the public and private sectors has notably improved. Since the State cannot always provide adequate financial support, the contribution of the private sector can partly substitute it. Besides his normal duties, the Superintendent, with his technical and scientific background, has gradually been transformed into a manager who has to try to resolve the problems faced by his institution with help from outside sources. This had already been seen in 1925 when Modigliani was director, in 1950 with Fernanda Wittgens and then with Franco Russoli and Carlo Bertelli. We are not referring here merely to exhibitions and restoration of works of art, but of direct intervention in the gallery, the driving force and originator of these initiatives.

In this fervour of innovative activity which seems to resemble what happened in Italy in the fifties, the Brera is attempting to re-establish itself, but not with a huge project that the term "grande Brera" might suggest. It aims to become a living museum, with the dual function of conservation and protection of its paintings and of the provision of those services that the public demands, from information resources to exhibitions and direct acquaintance with the contents of the gallery. This plan has now been put into operation and is closely linked with the scheme regarding Palazzo Citterio.

Thanks to the collaboration of the Amici di Brera, the Istituto Bancario San Paolo of Turin has allocated a considerable sum towards the completion of the work on the second building, the plans for which have been drawn up by the architect James Stirling. The Brera has received funds from the State, as well as from the Cariplo (Cassa Risparmio Provincie Lombarde), the Banca Popolare di Milano and the Banca del Monte. Work is being carried out in a number of parts of the gallery, in particular in order to comply with the safety regulations which the Ministry of the Interior has imposed on public buildings. While this work is going on it is hoped, with all the necessary precautions and despite the considerable difficulties involved, to leave as many paintings as is feasible on display.

In this way every effort will be made to give the greatest possible architectural unity to the different parts of the gallery, to maintain the illumination from skylights, to update the necessary technical services—such as the air conditioning which up to now has never existed and the fire alarms—and to resolve the problems of the lighting equipment.

The main art gallery will continue to be the Brera, with a clearly indicated itinerary for visitors to follow and adequate information resources. Those services which are strictly necessary will be retained, such as a photographic darkroom, a first-aid post, a bookshop and a snack bar, while Palazzo Citterio, besides the storerooms, temporary exhibitions and collections which have been donated, will house all the services available for public consultation and those connected with the Superintendency. The link from one building to the other must necessarily be through the Botanical Garden, which is located between them. Because of its historical importance, this too should be renovated as soon as possible. The work is to be carried out in stages and it is to be hoped that if FIO funds, ordinary ministerial funds and sponsors allow, it will be possible to finish what was started fifteen years ago in a relatively short time.

In recent years many paintings have been restored, including the *Saint Luke Polyptych* by Mantegna, *Saint Mark Preaching at Alexandria* by Gentile and Giovanni Bellini, the *Finding of the Body of Saint Mark* by Tintoretto and the *Virgin and Child* by Giovanni Bellini. In 1986 the large painting of the *Human Flood* by Pellizza da Volpedo was donated and there were many contributions by sponsors. In 1990, after the death of Maria Jesi, the last group of paintings from her collection arrived at the gallery. The statue of *Pomona* by Marino Marini was donated by bequest.

The Brera is still very much alive despite the problems it has had to face in the past because, as in the past, it has always managed to obtain help and summon up the necessary energy to keep open and satisfy the cultural requirements of the public. Today, although the difficulties are perhaps even greater in number and more varied in character, the demand for culture never ceases to grow and, following the necessary changes and improvements, this great art gallery will regain its former efficiency and prestige.

Lombard Painting from the Fourteenth Century to the End of the Sixteenth Century
Pietro C. Marani

The Brera Art Gallery developed largely thanks to a steady flow of works coming from the Napoleonic despoliation and then the acquisition during the nineteenth and twentieth centuries of works of art, especially frescoes, coming principally from historic buildings which were in a poor state of repair or threatened with demolition. Thus the richness and distinctive character of the Lombard art of the Trecento would not even be symbolically present if it had not been possible in the last fifty years to bring to the gallery the frescoes from the Oratory of the Porro family at Mocchirolo in 1949, donated by the owners, or in 1970 to purchase from a private collection the painting by Giovanni da Milano depicting *Christ Adored by the Angels*. Were it not for these two great works the gallery would not have any certain masterpieces to offer the visitor interested in Trecento art in Lombardy except for the fresco from the demolished church of Santa Maria dei Servi depicting *Saint Catherine*, in which the head has been damaged and which may be attributed to Giovanni de' Grassi. With this artist, however, the visitor would suddenly be thrust into the refined international atmosphere of the Visconti that characterised the period when work was starting on Milan Cathedral, and would be deprived of any works of art dating to the previous more autonomous period of Trecento painting in Lombardy.

Nor would the visitors' comprehension of the most authentic and original Lombard art have been aided by the presence of two other frescoes, removed in 1842 and 1847 from the same church of Santa Maria dei Servi and donated to the gallery, together with the one by Giovanni de' Grassi, in 1847. One of these, depicting the *Virgin and Child Enthroned and Two Donors*, which can be attributed to an anonymous artist of the end of the fourteenth century, is so badly damaged that it is impossible to attempt a proper critical study of it, while the other, the *Virgin and Child with Saint Catherine, Saint Ursula, Saint George and the Donor Teodorico da Coira*, attribut-

ed by an old epigraph (now destroyed) to Simone da Corbetta, is too naive, even although it emanates something of a fairy-tale atmosphere which perhaps derived from the contemporary tradition of manuscript illumination. The variegated art of Trecento Lombardy—which incorporated elements from Florence, Siena, Venice and north of the Alps and already possessed an individual style, imbued with naturalism and elegance—after its separation from the other schools of painting thanks to the Master of the Fissariga Tomb, then produced the works directly inspired by Giotto and his followers active in Lombardy so that it was no longer dependent on the Master of Mocchirolo himself and Giovanni da Milano. But this art is not adequately illustrated even by the works of these two artists which are to be found in the Brera.

The painting depicting *Christ the Judge* by Giovanni da Milano (Caversaccio, Como, active 1346-1369), while it reflects perfectly the personality of the artist—who must have been influenced by north Italian painters before coming into contact with the milieu of Giotto in Florence, where he painted the frescoes in the Rinuccini Chapel in Santa Croce and for which he received a payment in 1365—cannot, strictly speaking, be considered to be a Lombard work. In fact, it seems credible, given the Florentine source of a number of other paintings of which the original polyptych was formed and of which this superb painting was part (panels from this polyptych are now in Paris, Turin and London), that it may have come from Santa Maria degli Angeli in Florence (from where it may have then gone to the Abbey of San Giovanni Decollato del Sasso, near Arezzo). In effect, as a painting that was produced in Florence, it is in many ways similar to the frescoes in Santa Croce executed between 1306 and 1365.

Lombard art of the Trecento produced many of its own distinctive forms, above all in the great fresco cycles, in the miniature *L'Ouvraige de Lombardie*, to use the splendid title with which it became famous in Europe, and,

18

in part, in its sculpture. Hence the most inquisitive visitors will have to continue their journey back in time outside the Brera by visiting, at the very least, among the historical buildings of Milan, the church of San Gottardo in Corte (where there is a Giottesque *Crucifixion*), what remains in the church of Santa Maria di Brera and the Archbishop's Palace, and in Lombardy outside Milan, the Baptistry of Varese, the churches of Santa Maria Maggiore and Sant'Agostino in Bergamo, Sant'Abbondio in Como, the Abbey of Chiaravalle (*Stories of the Life of the Virgin*), Viboldone (a lunette of 1349) as well as the Visconti Oratory at Albizzate and the Oratory of Santo Stefano at Lentate.

The latter work has always been directly related to the decoration of the Oratory at Mocchirolo, a small village near Lentate sul Seveso (now in the Brera Gallery), if for no other reason than the belief that the patron must have been the same, at least on the basis of the Porro family's coat of arms, which appears in both cycles. In fact, in the Mocchirolo cycle, in the main panel to the right of the *Crucifixion*, appears Count Porro with his family; in the presence of an array of angels, he offers a model of the chapel to the Virgin. Stefano Porro, who was appointed count palatine in 1368 by Emperor Charles IV, is believed to have had this chapel decorated before building the Oratory of Santo Stefano at Lentate, where he probably intended to place his tomb. The conjecture that Stefano Porro was the patron of the Chapel of Mocchirolo (put forward for the first time by Carotti) would seem to be confirmed by the presence, on the left wall, of the *Marriage of Saint Catherine*, since this was the name of Count Porro's wife. The identification of Stefano Porro as the patron of the frescoes now in the Brera is mainly of relevance in relation to the date of execution of the cycle, which scholars place somewhere between 1360 and 1375. The former attribution of the frescoes to Giovanni da Milano suggested by Carotti himself, for example, has not been confirmed by the majority of later scholars. Toesca must be credited with having identified the artist as being one of the best painters of the Trecento in Lombardy; he progressed beyond the Giottesque influences which had been diffused in Lombardy, developing his style in a manner that recalled Tommaso da Modena or Giusto de' Menabuoi. His painting was cultured, refined and delicate, but also attentive to naturalistic elements, and he was to have followers. Echoes of his art are to be found in a *Crucifixion* in the Milanese church of San Marco, in the *Triumph of Saint Thomas* in Sant'Eustorgio, again in Milan, and also in two frescoes from the church of San Francesco in Bergamo.

The Bergamasque echo of the painter of Mocchirolo led to the suggestion that he might have been a certain "Petrus de Nova" who worked on the decoration of the apse of Santa Maria Maggiore in Bergamo from 1373 onwards, but who was absent for some months in 1378 in order to go to paint at "Moncayrolum" (Meli, 1967).

The identification of the painter of Mocchirolo as Pietro da Nova has recently been refuted (Travi, 1988), above all due to the difficulty of giving the frescoes in the Oratory such a late date. From a stylistic point of view they would appear to have been executed at least ten years earlier. The difficulty is, however, not so serious as it might seem, especially if a recent discovery in the archives is taken into consideration. This would appear to allow the true patron of the Oratory of Mocchirolo to be identified: in fact he was not Stefano Porro, but a relative of his, Lanfranco Porro, who belonged to another branch of the Porro family which was entitled to the Mocchirolo property and had also been an official of the Visconti and was, among other things, referendary of Regina della Scala in Bergamo in 1377. Here Lanfranco could have personally made contact with Pietro da Nova, from whom he might well have been able to commission the painting of the frescoes in his Oratory, thereby emulating his relative, Stefano (Galli, 1990).

The *Saint Euphemia* by Giovannino de' Grassi (last decade of the fourteenth century), which has already been referred to, for its refined Late Gothic style and evident association with the Visconti court which characterised the construction of the Cathedral (built from 1387 onwards; note the great architecture structure composed of spires, pinnacles, mullioned windows and buttresses), could certainly constitute the link with the Milanese painting in the first half of the Quattrocento. Perhaps no other work could reflect better than the Visconti *Tarot Cards* the extremely refined and cultured court atmosphere which permeated Milanese art in the second quarter of the century. Besides the Brera pack, purchased by the State in 1971 (from the collection of Giovanni Brambilla, who had bought it in Venice at the beginning of this century) and consisting of forty-eight cards, two other packs are known to us (the Visconti di Modrone pack, now at Yale University, New Haven; and the Colleoni-Baglioni pack, now divided between the Accademia Carrara in Bergamo and the Pierpont Morgan Library in New York), which are both incomplete (a complete tarot pack contains seventy-eight cards) and can both be attributed to the same workshop (Bandera, 1988).

In these cards can be seen the influence of the International Gothic style, which was made fashionable in Lombardy by, among others, Gentile da Fabriano (frescoes almost totally lost in the Broletto in Brescia, 1414-19), as well as by Michelino da Besozzo, through whom the language of the Lombard manuscript illuminators was enriched with Northern accents. The gallery owns two other small cuspidated paintings by Bonifacio Bembo, depicting *Saint Alexis and Saint Julian* (or *Saint James*), donated by Count Paolo Gerli di Villagaeta in 1950. Of a later date than the *Tarot Cards*, c. 1465-70?, the refined and meticulously-finished figures of saints — which should not be considered to be parts of a polyptych, but rather as single paintings — may have been executed for the Chapel of the

20

Reliquaries in Pavia Castle. This was one of the most mysterious undertakings in the history of Lombard art, which involved, not only Bembo, but also Giovanni Vismara, Vincenzo Foppa and the elusive Zanetto Bugatto. Absolutely nothing remains of it, even though there are inventories of reliquaries from the enterprise which were still stored in Milan Cathedral in 1499.

The childlike tone of the images in the Brambilla tarot cards, with at times influence of Pisanello's manner and excessive attention to the sumptuous but vacuous world of the court, seems to be a forerunner of the bewildered, dreamy air of the fresco figures of the Zavattari in the Chapel of Teodolinda in Monza Cathedral. The *Portrait of Francesco Sforza* and the *Portrait of Bianca Maria Sforza* came from the Chapter of Monza Cathedral (donated to the gallery in 1932 by the Amici di Brera); until recently they were attributed to Bonifacio Bembo, who was thought to have painted them late in his career. But the enormous difference in dimensions and style compared to the *Tarot Cards* has now caused the traditional attribution to be excluded (nor is the alternative suggestion that the artist might be Benedetto Bembo acceptable), particularly because there is an atmosphere that is excessively celebratory, which would have been unsuitable for the political climate in which it is supposed that these works were executed, that is to say under the rule of Galeazzo Maria Sforza. Therefore it appears more logical to think that the two portraits must have been painted rather later, after 1480, on the initiative of Ludovico Sforza, who intended to celebrate his dynasty by commemorating its founder. The execution and style of the paintings (as well as the style of the costume) are not an obstacle to this new date, which is now confirmed by distinguished precedents and by the tradition of the "diptych" portrait which Piero della Francesca made popular with the portraits of the Duke and Duchess of Urbino (Uffizi, Florence).

The panel painting in tempera which depicts the *Assumption of the Virgin* (donated to the gallery by the heirs of Paolo Gerli in 1982) may be attributed to one of the Zavattari. This painting fully expresses the illustrative and childlike atmosphere and taste which held sway at the Visconti court in the mid-fifteenth century (the decoration of the Chapel of Teodolinda in Monza Cathedral, with which the painting is linked stylistically, was completed in 1444). The Late Gothic tradition to which the Zavattari belonged was to continue through the second half of the Quattrocento, as is demonstrated, for example, by the works of Bernardino Butinone (Treviglio, c. 1450-1507) such as the triptych with *Virgin and Child and Saint Leonard and Saint Bernardino*, although this was contemporary with the development of new tendencies regarding the use of space and composition. Butinone showed, both here and later on (as in the delicate *Virgin and Child* purchased in 1901, which was perhaps one of his last works), that he wanted to abandon the Paduan-Ferrarese archaism and adapt himself to the new more monumental and robust style of Vincenzo Foppa.

This artist (Brescia, c. 1472-c. 1515), who may well be considered one of the great masters of the Renaissance in the Po Valley, is represented in the gallery by the imposing polyptych from the church of Santa Maria delle Grazie in Bergamo (it came to the Brera in 1811). Even though the perspective was not unified and centralised, as would be the case shortly afterwards in the Treviglio polyptych, executed from 1485 onwards by Butinone and Zenale, this work is remarkable for the attempt to give a sense of illusionistic depth to the two-dimensional pictorial surface and for "its renewed feeling for chiaroscuro" (Natale, 1988), as well as for the profound sense of humanity and spiritual involvement which it emanates. The very recent restoration (1991) of the fifteen panels which form the polyptych (it was, however, arbitrarily recomposed in the nineteenth century) allows its purely pictorial qualities to be fully appreciated. Thus it can be considered one of

22   the fundamental paintings in Lombardy at a date which was crucial, but which was from many points of view problematic, that is to say 1483, to which reference has already been made. Two other extraordinary frescoes by Foppa (*Virgin and Child with Saint John the Baptist and Saint John the Evangelist*, dated 10 October 1485, and the *Martyrdom of San Sebastian*, both removed from the church of Santa Maria di Brera) display a free application of centralised perspective which favours illusionistic and scenographic effects rather than rigidly optical and geometrical ones.

The other important artist present in Milan in the second half of the Quattrocento, Bernardo Zenale (Treviglio, 1436–Milan, 1523), who like Foppa was fascinated by architecture, to such an extent that he became an architect in the latter part of his life. He is represented in the gallery by a *Virgin and Child with Two Angels Playing Music* (purchased in 1910), painted early in the Cinquecento, in which should be noted the trompe l'oeil of the two angels who protrude from the surface of the painting, and the *Virgin and Child* formerly in the Noseda collection (at the Brera since 1978 after being purchased), in which there may be the hand of other artists, and in which the influence of Leonardo, Bergognone and Flemish painters is also evident.

The more typically Lombard and personal vein of Ambrogio Bergognone (Milan?, c. 1453-Milan, 1523) can be noted in the fresco removed from the church of Santa Maria dei Servi in 1847, depicting the *Virgin and Child, Four Angels and God the Father* (the bust and head of God the Father were destroyed during the removal of the fresco) and the enchanting small painting representing the *Virgin and Child with Saint Catherine of Siena and a Carthusian Monk* (purchased in 1891), which are the two oldest paintings of his at the Brera (c. 1480-90). In this work it is possible to observe the peaceful, dark lyricism for which Bergognone is rightly famous and which is only slightly illuminated by gleams of light that range from a cold Northern glitter to a more golden Mediterranean glow.

The artist was to change his palette and spatial scale, while holding fast to his tenets in his highly illustrative poetic style, after the arrival in Lombardy of Bramante and Leonardo. Perspective illusionism and a greater monumental scale for his figures already permeated the frescoes in the Certosa di Pavia (on which he worked without interruption continuously from 1488 to 1494), but they can be clearly observed also in the cycle of frescoes from the transept in San Satiro, now in the Brera (ten frescoes removed in the nineteenth century), where figures of female saints stand out with illusionistic effect in loggias which open onto a blue sky. There is a clear intention to create an illusionistic sense of depth to pictorial space which was suggested by none other than Bramante, who worked in the same church on the false perspective of the choir. On the other hand evidence of the discovery of the Leonardesque aesthetic ideal of the sfumato is seen in the *Virgin with Sleeping Child* (also called *Virgin of the Veil*, purchased in 1911), and in part, given that there are elements of Flemish culture, the *Ecce Homo* (from the Sipriot collection, 1903), while in his last painting, the altarpiece depicting the *Assumption of the Virgin*, from the church of Santa Maria Incoronata at Nerviano (at the Brera since 1809), dated 1522, he appears to return, even though somewhat wearily, to his original style of simple popular illustrator. With Bergognone it really does seem that as Roberto Longhi wrote "the last great poetic expression of the Lombard Quattrocento" faded away.

The arrival of Bramante on the Milanese artistic scene (he was already present in Bergamo towards the end of the 1480s) was to have a profound influence. This was not so much due to his paintings as to, on the one hand, the introduction of the geometrical and mathematical values of the culture of Urbino he had carried out (these implied a total rethinking, for example, of architectural design) and, on the other hand, for the consequences that his influence could have on a Lombard artist like

Bernardo Zenale, Virgin and Child with Two Angels Playing Music.

Ambrogio Bergognone, Virgin and Child with Saint Catherine of Siena and a Carthusian Monk.

Bramantino. An absolutely unique example of the art of Bramante (Monte Asdruvaldo, Fermignano, 1444-Rome, 1514) is the *Christ at the Column* (on loan from the Abbey of Chiaravalle since 1915), which is admirable for its sense of pathos and the rounded, sculpturesque volume of the figure. These elements, added to a three-dimensional and very lucid vision of reality, cause it to be a truly revolutionary work for Milan in the last decade of the fifteenth century. Although we must not forget its debts to Melozzo da Forlì, it can only bear comparison with the calmly imposing apse of San Satiro. Less successful from a pictorial point of view—but it is necessary to remember the vicissitudes and restoration these works have been subjected to—appear, therefore, the *Men-at-arms*, eight frescoes removed from the Casa Visconti, later Panigarola, in Milan (at the Brera since 1901-02), in which Bramante once again affirmed his illusionistic and scenographic ideals. Indeed he took these ideals to their extreme consequences by depicting the figures of the *Men-at-arms* in large niches, the bases of which are moved perilously upwards, to the limit of verisimilitude. Perhaps this is an allegorical representation of the "perfect state" according to a Neo-Platonic vision of life linked to the cult of the "hero" diffused by Ficino (in the fragment with *Heraclitus and Democritus* are said to be represented the opposite attitudes of life, tears and laughter). The cycle of frescoes was probably painted around 1487, when Bramante frequented the house of Gasparo Ambrogio Visconti, a warrior and poet at the court of the Sforza. For this reason among the "heroes" is perhaps also portrayed a poet, the so-called *Singer*.

One of the most unusual products of Lombard art, in which there is an unsuccessful attempt to merge the two new trends imposed on Milanese artists by Bramante and Leonardo in the last two decades of the Quattrocento, must certainly be the *Pala Sforzesca*. In this intricate painting Ludovico il Moro and his family pay homage to the *Virgin and Child* and the *Four Doctors of the Church*. It came

Donato Bramante, Christ at the Column.

to the Brera in 1808 from the church of Sant' Ambrogio ad Nemus in Milan with an authoritative, but incorrect, attribution to Leonardo, while in fact it is the crucial work of an anonymous artist (active until around 1520) who is given, on the basis of this painting, the name of Master of the Pala Sforzesca. Obliged as he was to respect a preordained iconography (in a document of 1494 the artist submitted a description of the painting to the Duke), the artist demonstrated the conflict between the local tradition—there are references to Foppa, Butinone, Bergognone and Zenale and also to the sculptor Mantegazza— and the new stylistic dictates, in other words the sfumato of Leonardesque origin and the spatial structure which recalls Bramante even though it was familiar to Bergognone too, adapted to the tastes of a court whose official painters were de' Predis and Bernardino de' Conti. The result is that passages of the painting which are superficially descriptive and executed in a somewhat crude manner alternate with delightful passages where the paint is handled delicately, thus rendering the work the classic product of an artist who had not yet decided how he should develop from a stylistic point of view.

On the other hand Bartolomeo Suardi, known as Bramantino (Milan, c. 1465-1530) had already made up his mind. After being influenced by Butinone and the Ferrarese school he turned his attention without hesitation to Bramante, relying on his innate capacity for transformation and synthesis. The huge painting of the *Crucifixion* (of uncertain provenance, it was already in the Brera in 1806) is one of the greatest achievements of his career. It oscillates between severe classicism (which he had picked up in Rome, possibly at the end of the Quattrocento and the beginning of the Cinquecento or then, certainly, in 1508-1509) and bizarre imaginary architecture, but is always sustained by rigorous perspective and a modular structure which serves as a "cage" within which the figures can be arranged in space. The recent

restoration and the analyses with radiography and infra-red reflectography carried out on this painting (1991) have shown that the original formulation of the theme was very different. In particular there was an enormous building in the background, perhaps based on Castel Sant'Angelo in Rome, which was then eliminated in the final version, perhaps as a result of requests from reformist circles in Milan. The *Virgin and Child and a Male Figure* (from the collection of Cardinal Cesare Monti, where it had been present since c. 1650) and the *Virgin and Child and Two Angels* (detached fresco from the Palazzo della Ragione in Piazza Mercanti, Milan, in the Brera since 1808), both display, despite the differences in format and support, the desire to produce monumental forms which are frozen, almost compressed in space and, at the same time, the interest taken by Bramantino in the Leonardesque ideas concerning optics and light. Bramantino's works, with their brilliant intellectual vision, had a vast following among Lombard artists and constituted the most original answer to the domination of the Leonardesque school in the early part of the Cinquecento.

The "school," but it would be better to speak of the "followers," that Leonardo had in Lombardy, is represented in the Brera by a notable series of panel paintings and a considerable number of detached frescoes. Giovanni Ambrogio de' Predis (Milan, c. 1455-1508 and after) fluctuated somewhat between court archaism and full commitment to the new developments, but his *Portrait of a Young Man* (purchased in 1914), although it is too immobile and crystallized, is one of his best answers to the new course of events (it imitates the *Portrait of a Musician* by Leonardo at the Ambrosiana). Among the artists who were most directly affected by the new art, based as it was on the sfumato and a vision that was internalized and rich in psychological implications, and documented as being present in Leonardo's workshop in the last decade of the fifteenth century, were, be-

Donato Bramante, Heraclitus and Democritus.

Bartolomeo Suardi, called il Bramantino,
Crucifixion.

sides Ambrogio de' Predis (who had collaborated with Leonardo on the Virgin of the Rocks (Louvre, Paris and National Gallery, London), were Giovanni Antonio Boltraffio and Marco d'Oggiono. The former (Milan, 1467-1516) painted the *Portrait of Gerolamo Casio* (it came from the Biblioteca Universitaria in Bologna in 1902), while Marco (Oggiono, near Como, 1475-Milano, 1530?) should at least be remembered for the large altarpiece depicting *Three Archangels* (from the church of Santa Marta in Milan, at the Brera since 1808). Although it has been subjected to a lot of criticism because of its excessive complexity and the incongruous gestures and draperies, this painting reveals the sophisticated technique which Marco had attained (with a landscape background that is certainly no mean achievement) and the new unifying vision of space "without perspective," introduced by Leonardo in his altarpieces. Marco d'Oggiono's output is often repetitive and monotonous (see the *Assumption of the Virgin*, in the Brera since 1809, and the *Assumption of the Magdalen*, in the Brera since 1988), but the smaller paintings, such as the *Virgin and Child* (formerly Vonmiller, in the Brera since 1935) manage to provide a more engaging expression of the artist's feelings.

Among his closest followers is worthy of mention Francesco Napoletano (who had previously been identified as a Lombard painter, Francesco Galli, active in the early years of the 500). He was responsible for a remarkable *Virgin and Child* (in the Brera since 1883 as the result of an exchange), which was clearly influenced by Leonardo's *Benois Madonna* (Hermitage, St. Petersburg). However, of the artists who were endowed with much greater personality who were able to link Leonardo with their varied experience, pride of place must be given to Andrea Solario (Milan, 1468/70-1524), Giovanni Agostino da Lodi (Lodi, last decade of the fifteenth century—until c. 1520), Cesare da Sesto (Sesto Calende, 1477-Milan, 1523) and Bernardino Luini (Luino?, c. 1480-Milan, 1532). The *Virgin and Child with Saint Joseph and Saint*

Giovanni Agostino da Lodi, Apostles.
Altobello Melone, Portrait of Alda Gambara.

Simeon by Solario, dated 1495 (from the church of San Pietro Martire at Murano, in the Brera since 1811), the *Virgin and Child* from San Pasquale Baylon in Venice (in the Brera since 1808), as well as the *Portrait of a Young Man* (from the Monti collection, in the Brera since 1811), are clear evidence of the extent to which Solario had been influenced by his stay in Venice, where he was able to come into contact with the art Alvise Vivarini and, possibly, with that of Dürer.

The two *Apostles* by Giovanni Agostino da Lodi (purchased 1913), perhaps executed in Venice immediately after 1495, display the influence of both Bramante and Leonardo, while the *Virgin and Child* by Cesare da Sesto (in the Brera since 1824) add an elegant Raphaelesque touch to the Leonardesque sfumato. But it was Luini who provided the freshest and most spontaneous interpretation of the Leonardesque style in Milan and Lombardy. Rather than in easel-painting, although the *Virgin of the Rose Garden* (purchased 1825) is noteworthy for its extraordinary pictorial quality, he displayed these gifts of his in fresco painting. In the Brera there are the frescoes removed (between 1805 and 1875) from the Chapel of San Giuseppe in the church of Santa Maria della Pace and recomposed in the Brera from 1901 to 1903, and many of those from Villa La Pelucca, formerly of the Rabia family, in Sesto San Giovanni (in the Brera since 1826). The latter is a fresco cycle which is of the greatest possible iconographic interest in that it appears to illustrate episodes from the history of the Jews (Ferri Piccaluga, 1989). A scene like the one of the *Bathing Maidens* might well be considered emblematic of the refined intimacy of Luini's classicism. Indeed this is a scene which must have fascinated both Puvis de Chavannes and Renoir, and which may partly explain why the artist was so popular in the nineteenth century.

Worthy of mention among the late followers of Leonardo is the artist known as Giampietrino, who has now been identified as Giovan Pietro Rizzoli (Lombardy, active from

1520 to 1549), who painted refined easel-paintings that depicted, in general, wan Mary Magdelenes, such as the two in the Brera collection (*Mary Magdelene Seated in Prayer*, purchased 1835, and a *Half-length Figure of Mary Magdelene* from the Monti collection, in the Brera since 1811). Of lesser importance is Cesare Magni, who was present in Milan between 1530 and 1533 (see his *Holy Family*, from the Monti collection, 1811, painted in a lifeless Leonardesque manner and based more on Cesare da Sesto). A painting by a follower of Leonardo whose attribution is still open to debate is the *Virgin and Child with a Lamb* (purchased 1891). Derived from Leonardo's studies for the *Virgin with the Cat*, it was previously believed to be by a Lombard artist, but has recently been attributed to Fernando Yáñez de Almedina, who was perhaps the artist who helped Leonardo in Florence with the painting of the *Battle of Anghiari*. However, Fernando was not able to produce painting of this standard and so the problem has yet to be solved. The artist must have had access to Leonardo's drawings, which were often used for painting copies which were not always very precise. A partial copy of the Leonardo's *Virgin of the Rocks* present in the Brera is by Bernardino de' Conti (Cereda Rovelli gift, 1899), signed by the artist and dated 1522. It is a retardataire work which seems to ignore the development of Mannerism that was taking place in Lombardy at the time.

The number of Lombard artists grew considerably in the first half of the Cinquecento if those working outside Milan are taken into consideration, especially in Lodi and Cremona. The Brera has two paintings by Martino and Albertino Piazza da Lodi: by Albertino (Lodi and Milan, active until 1529) there is a *Crucifixion of Saint Peter* (purchased 1906), by Martino (Lodi and Milan, active until 1527) a monumental and powerful *Saint John the Baptist* (in the Brera since 1805). Worthy of note by the most important artist in Lodi, Calisto Piazza (Lodi, 1500-1562) is a large painting depicting the *Virgin and Child with*

Saint John the Baptist and Saint Jerome (from San Francesco in Brescia, in the Brera since 1829) in which there are Ferrarese and, in particular, Brescian influences, from Dosso Dossi to Moretto, and a *Baptism of Christ* (from Santa Caterina in Crema, 1811) where, however, he appears to pay more attention to the influence of Venetian painting, as well as that of Gaudenzio Ferrari. From Cremona there is the *Virgin and Child with a Bird* by Boccaccio Boccaccino (Cremona, c. 1465-1524/25) and the *Virgin and Child between Saint Blaise and Saint Anthony Abbot* by Galeazzo Campi (Cremona, 1477-1536), both works in which Venetian and Bellinesque influences are evident. Then there are two important paintings by Altobello Melone (Cremona, c. 1485-before 1543): a *Deposition* (purchased 1916), strongly influenced by Bramantino, and the *Portrait of Alda Gambara*, formerly in the Trivulzio collection, from where it went to England; it was recovered by Siviero and has been in the Brera since 1988. Representing a decisive, monumental figure echoed by Brescia Castle, which is depicted in the background, this painting had previously been unjustifiably attributed to Boltraffio and Bartolomeo Veneto.

The artistic scene in Lombardy in the first half of the Cinquecento also benefited from the presence of a number of "foreign" artists: Gaudenzio Ferrari, active in Milan and the surrounding area (Busto Arsizio, Saronno) and Bernardino Lanino.

Gaudenzio (Valduggia, Vercelli, c. 1480-Milan, 1546) was responsible for the *Virgin and Child*, part of a dismembered polyptych (from the Savoy collections, purchased 1890), in which he appears to be measuring himself with the Leonardesque "impulse of the spirit"; the large *Martyrdom of Saint Catherine* (from the church of Sant'Angelo in Milan, in the Brera since 1829), which is more superficial and seems almost to be a scene from the "great mountain theatre"; and the cycle of frescoes removed from the Chapel of the Natività della Vergine in the church of Santa Maria della Pace (in the Brera since 1808),

Vincenzo Campi, Fish-monger, detail.

Antonio Campi, Virgin and Child with Saint Catherine and Saint Agnes.

Sofonisba Anguissola, Self-portrait.

where, unexpectedly, in the panel with the *Annunciation*, in the backdrop of a city with towers and domes, the surreal poetry of Bramantino seems to be present once again.

These works were decisive in Lombardy in the late Cinquecento for the creation of a new style that was more verist and dramatic and, even more so, for the "painters of reality" in Lombardy during the Seicento. Lanino was the other great "foreigner" (Vercelli, 1512-1583), but he was, however, milder and more superficial than Gaudenzio; he was attributed with a freely adapted copy of the *Virgin and Child with Saint Anne* (from the Collegio di Sant'Alessandro in Milan, 1810), which with its brilliant colours is clear evidence, notwithstanding the homage which is paid to Leonardo, of the change in atmosphere and tastes in Milan around 1540.

Milanese art in the second half of the Cinquecento was, with the exception of Cremona, practically synonymous with Lombard art because, in fact, the cities of Bergamo and Brescia were in the sphere of influence of Venetian painting. Perhaps its most emblematic painting was the *Self-portrait* by Giovan Paolo Lomazzo (Milan, 1538-1600), who was the author of the first theoretical treatise in the history of Milanese art, which may be compared with Vasari's work on Tuscan art. In the *Self-portrait* (purchased 1821), executed before 1570, Lomazzo seems to have been influenced by Leonardo on the one hand and Giorgione on the other (two of the most important names, in fact, in North Italian art), disguising them, however, with a vernacular style that is almost playful in nature, thereby foreshadowing genre painting. Indeed it is the latter that seems to have been diffused in Cremona, also due to the contribution of the Dutch painters, with the paintings by Vincenzo Campi (Cremona, 1536-1591), *Fruitseller* and *Fishmonger* (from the Monastery of the Gerolomiti di San Sigismondo in Cremona, in the Brera since 1809; two analogous paintings are in the Brera Academy). But painting in Cremona in the second half of the century is represented, above all, by the

works of Giulio Campi (Cremona, c. 1508-1573), Antonio Campi (Cremona, 1522/23-1587)—note his large *Virgin and Child with Saint Catherine and Saint Agnes* from the church of San Barnaba in Milan, in the Brera since 1810—and Bernardino Campi (Reggio Emilia, 1519-1591) whose large *Pietà with Saint Catherine of Alexandria and the Prophets Elijah and Elisha and Gabriele Quintiano* is also in the Brera (from the church of the Carmelitani in Crema, 1811). In this painting Bernardino's aristocratic manner is toned down by a more emotional involvement in the drama; it was partially copied by his pupil, Sofonisba Anguissola (Cremona, 1522/23-Palermo, 1626) on a small panel, which is also in the Brera (purchased 1909). There is also a refined *Self-portrait* (purchased 1911), which was probably executed in Spain around 1560 by this cultured aristocratic lady painter, who was a meticulous illustrator of court life in Europe and was in correspondence with the great Michelangelo (from whom she copied a sizable number of drawings).

With the works of these Lombard Mannerists, imbued in refinement and sophistry, the development of the most authentic Lombard art seems to have ground to halt. The guiding theme of naturalism and the cold silvery tones that were so typical of it had been interrupted. This theme, which can be traced from as far back as the Master of the Oratory of Mocchirolo and included such outstanding artists as Foppa, Bergognone, Zenale and Bramantino, would have to await the arrival of the "painters of the plague" in order to be taken up once again.

Painting in Lombardy in the Seventeenth and Eighteenth Centuries
Simonetta Coppa

The collection of seventeenth and eighteenth century Lombard paintings in the Brera Gallery is noteworthy both from the point of view of quantity and from that of quality. The gallery was initially conceived as part of a precise programme of the imperial cultural policy, with the intention of documenting through carefully selected examples the development of the various schools of painting that existed in the Napoleonic Kingdom of Italy, as far as its status as the National Gallery of the capital city of the Kingdom would allow. However, the decisive contribution to the formation of the Brera collection, beginning with the first group of paintings which was put together for purposes that were primarily of an educational nature in the rooms of the Brera Academy by Abbot Carlo Bianconi, secretary from 1778 to 1801, derived from the massive phenomenon of dissolution of religious bodies which took place in Lombardy under Austrian rule in the last decades of the eighteenth century as part of the reforms carried out by Maria Theresa and Joseph. These reforms continued under Napoleon and culminated in the decree which dissolved all the religious orders. For example, when Bianconi was secretary the paintings from the church of Santi Cosma e Damiano alla Scala in Milan came to the Brera; they included works by Giuseppe Nuvolone and Legnanino and four altarpieces by Batoni, Bottoni and Subleyras, who played a fundamental role in diffusing classicism in the local artistic milieu.

Although the expropriations in the various departments of the Kingdom by the Napoleonic commissioners were carried out with the intention of concentrating in the Milan Art Gallery outstanding works from different schools of painting in all the phases of their stylistic and chronological development, since they obtained works from the great reserve of suppressed churches it was inevitable that a considerable quantity of Seicento and Settecento paintings from Lombardy poured into the Brera. Milan had been profoundly affected by the reformism of Charles and Federico Borromeo; in the age of the Counter-Reformation the heritage of works of art and historical buildings in the city was radically expanded and renewed, and this then continued right through the Seicento and Settecento. It was duly reported in the local literature and guides, including Morigia (1595), Borsieri (1619), Santagostino (1671), Torre (1674) and Latuada (1737-38) right up to the *Nuova guida di Milano* by Bianconi, whose two editions (1787 and 1795) were written during the period of the suppressions.

The renewal extended from the city to the diocese, involving not only the places which were of such great importance for the religious devotions during the Counter-Reformation and Baroque period, the great shrines dedicated to the Virgin Mary and the Sacri Monti, but also following the itineraries of the pastoral visits, thereby reaching the remotest villages in the rural and mountain parishes. Charles Borromeo's episcopate soon became the post-Tridentine model, and the example which he provided in the encouragement of the arts was emulated not only by his successors in the Milan diocese, from his cousin Federico to Cesare Monti, both connoisseurs and keen collectors, to Giuseppe Pozzobonelli in the sixteenth century, but also in the neighbouring Lombard dioceses which were to a large extent suffragan to the Milanese one.

The *Virgin and Child with Saint John the Evangelist and Saint Michael* by Ambrogio Figino, an altarpiece from the chapel of the Collegio dei Dottori in Milan, lauded shortly after its execution in the dialogue *Il Figino* by Comanino (1591), is evidence of the influence on the painter, who was an important follower of Late Mannerism in Milan, of Raphaelesque and Michelangelesque styles, as interpreted by Pellegrino Tibaldi, while the atmosphere of gloomy chiaroscuro which envelops the figures is of Leonardesque origin. The two *Franciscan Stories* by Giovanni Battista Crespi, called Cerano, (*Saint Francis Freeing the Prisoner* and *Saint Francis Healing the Leper*) together with another

36

two panels now in the Civici Musei in the Castello Sforzesco in Milan, are believed by scholars to have formed part of the altarpiece depicting the *Vows of the Franciscan Saints* painted in 1600 for the Capuchin church of the Immacolata in Milan (formerly in the Berlin Museums, destroyed in 1945). The narrative quality, the intense expressiveness and the density of the layer of paint "which directly exploits the texture of the support to create effects of vibrant light" (Rosci, in *Pinacoteca di Brera...*, 1989, p. 92) all indicate how distant Cerano was from the styles of Gaudenzio Ferrari and the Mannerists and that a new era had begun with his art which was to culminate in the enormous paintings depicting Saint Charles Borromeo in Milan Cathedral. A good example of Counter-Reformation piety which became popular during the episcopate of Federico Borromeo due to his austere religious zeal is the altarpiece of the *Virgin of the Rosary with Saint Dominic and Saint Catherine*, formerly on the high altar of the church belonging to the Dominican nuns of San Lazzaro alle Monache in Milan. Since the frescoes by Panfilo Nuvolone which surrounded the altarpiece are documented as having been executed between 1618 and 1621, it is reasonable to date the work by Cerano towards the end of the second decade of the seventeenth century, just before the foundation of the Accademia Ambrosiana by Federico Borromeo, where Cerano became a teacher of painting.

The depiction of a half-length figure of Saint Francis in the ecstasy of the stigmatization, in the gesture of displaying the wounds or contemplating the crucifix is frequent in Milanese painting in the early Seicento, and this is parallel with what was happening at the same time in Spanish painting. Cerano, in the painting which was donated to the Brera in 1969 by Ruggero Poletti, offers a psychological interpretation of his theme without the contrived expressiveness which is typical of the paintings of Saint Francis by Morazzone and Cairo, presenting the saint as a "friar who was still quite young, who had become

thin and livid as a result of his penance, but was substantially aristocratic, with a basis of self-awareness which resisted total abandonment" (Rosci, 1964, p. 100). The work is the prototype of a successful series of derivatives by the artist and his school, to which belongs also the painting by Ortensio Crespi, his brother.

More dramatic in its harsh realism and violence of the contrasts of light and shade is the interpretation of Morazzone, in a painting which was generally considered to be a late work, but the analogies with frescoes of the Cappella della Flagellazione at the Sacro Monte of Varese induced Gregori (1962) to date it towards the end of the first decade of the Seicento. To the last years of the painter, who died in 1625, belongs the *Saint Anthony Abbot and Saint Paul the Hermit*, from the collection of Cardinal Cesare Monti, stylistically and typologically similar to the monastic saints in the Cappella della Buona Morte in the church of San Gaudenzio in Novara.

Compared with the divine inspiration of Cerano and Morazzone, the painting of Giulio Cesare Procaccini is characterised by a heightened effusion of sentiment due to the influence on the one hand of Tuscan and Emilian Mannerism, on the other hand of Rubens and the Genoese school. Seicento and Settecento sources refer to his sojourn in Genoa in 1618, and recent studies (Brigstocke, 1988) have brought to light on the basis of documentary evidence the importance of the patronage of Gian Carlo Doria, for whom Giulio Cesare Procaccini executed over sixty paintings. The *Saint Charles, Dead Christ and an Angel*, formerly an altarpiece in the church of Santa Giustina e San Carlo in Pavia, which was rebuilt by Basilian monks and consecrated in 1613, is inspired by a vision of the saint at the Sacro Monte at Varallo, a subject which was frequent in the iconography relating to Saint Charles in the Seicento.

While from a thematic point of view Procaccini was influenced by the example of the *Dead Christ Adored by Saint Charles and other Saints* by Cerano in the church of Santo Ste-

Giovanni Battista Crespi called il Cerano, Virgin of the Rosary with Saint Dominic and Saint Catherine.

fano in Milan, he reinterprets it, moreover in his own manner, countering Cerano's austere and well-coordinated sense of tragedy with the highly charged emotional fire of the dialogue between Saint Charles and the angel. Also the theme of the *Glory of Saint Charles* is among the most popular in Lombard painting in the period of Federico Borromeo. Procaccini, in an altarpiece for the Genoese church of San Francesco d'Albaro provides a proto-Baroque version that is bright and triumphant and which shows traces both of Rubens's exuberant use of colour and the scintillating iridescence of Parmigianino and Mazzola Bedoli.

The *Mystic Marriage of Saint Catherine* and the *Mary Magdalen*, both formerly in the collection of Cardinal Monti, are refined examples of paintings executed for hanging in private houses, in which the grace of the figures, the carefully studied perfection of the handling of the paint and the psychological atmosphere which varies from smiling tenderness to weary morbidity, derive once again from Emilian roots, ranging from Correggio to Parmigianino.

Among the most unusual paintings of the Seicento in Lombardy is the *Martyrdom of Saint Rufina and Saint Seconda*, better known as the "three-handed picture," the result of the collaboration between Cerano (who painted the left-hand part with the warrior on horseback and the beheaded Saint Seconda), Morazzone (who was responsible for the executioner in the centre, the two soldiers and the angel in the background and, perhaps, the overall planning of the composition) and Giulio Cesare Procaccini (who produced Saint Rufina and the angel on the right). The work was commissioned around 1620-25 by Scipione Toso, a Milanese gentleman and collector, perhaps on the recommendation of Girolamo Borsieri. After the death of Toso it went to the collection of Cardinal Cesare Monti; it was mentioned for the first time in 1625, while Giovanni Pasta gave it the title of "three-handed painting" in 1636.

Giulio Cesare's elder brother, Camillo Procaccini, came to Milan in 1587 from Emilia after a journey to Rome as part of his education as a painter which was facilitated by the patronage of Pirro Visconti. He was a follower of an artistic current with intellectual and academic overtones which sought its inspiration both in the Late Mannerism of Tuscany and Rome and in Pellegrino Tibaldi, an artist who had successfully countered the sentimentalism of Cerano and Morazzone. Camillo remained firmly rooted to these origins during his long career in Lombardy, as is demonstrated by the *Adoration of the Shepherds*, which clearly showed the influence of Correggio and was painted around 1615 for the Franciscan church of Santa Maria del Giardino in Milan.

For Giuseppe Vermiglio and Tanzio da Varallo the journeys to Rome and, in Tanzio's case, also to Central and Southern Italy were an opportunity for closer contact with Caravaggesque naturalism and light effects. Thus these stimulating ideas which were conveyed by them helped to enliven the artistic scene in Lombardy and Piedmont in the early part of the Seicento. Signed and dated 1622, the *Adoration of the Shepherds* for the church of Santa Maria delle Grazie in Novara was a key work by Vermiglio shortly after his return from Rome and was a synthesis of Caravaggism and Emilian art.

The *Martyrdom of the Franciscans in Nagasaki* by Tanzio, from the Convento delle Grazie at Varallo, proposes a theme which was a burning issue at the time. The painting combines influences of Ceranesque mannerism with direct references to the *Crucifixion of Saint Peter* by Caravaggio in Santa Maria del Popolo in Rome.

Although Daniele Crespi's point of departure was Late Lombard Mannerism (he was a pupil of Cerano at the Accademia Ambrosiana), he was able to attain a synthesis of Emilian classicism and Caravaggesque naturalism, which the brevity of his life (he was a victim of the plague epidemic in 1630, when he was just over thirty years old) prevented him from developing completely. The *Way to Calvary*,

donated by Cardinal Cesare Monti to the Senate of Milan and formerly hanging in the meeting chamber of the Ducal Palace, still abounds with references to Cerano, Morazzone and Giulio Cesare Procaccini in the composition which is constructed on a network of diagonals giving prominence to the figure of Christ. It formed the beginning of a cycle of *Stories of the Passion of Christ*, executed in the second half of the Seicento by Stefano Montalto, Ercole Procaccini il Giovane, Carlo Cornara, Antonio Busca, Giuseppe Nuvolone and Agostino Santagostino. Among the masterpieces of his mature period was the *Last Supper* from the church of the Benedictine convent of Santa Maria at Brugora in Brianza, where it was the altarpiece on the high altar. It is a reworking of an invention by Gaudenzio Ferrari in the *Last Supper* in Santa Maria della Passione in Milan "in the arrangement of the figures along a longitudinal axis seen from a raised viewpoint with windows opening in the architecture behind" (Bora, in *Pinacoteca di Brera...*, 1989, p. 213). The lightening of his palette, which was distancing itself from the strong contrasts of chiaroscuro which were so typical of the Lombard Seicento, the deep expressiveness and the complete comprehensibility indicate an opening towards Emilian naturalistic classicism and place the painting just before the cycles in the Certosa di Garegnano and the Certosa di Pavia.

The *Baptism of Christ*, from the Franciscan church of Santa Maria delle Grazie in Monza, also belongs to his mature years. It too reworks a Cinquecentesque model of Leonardesque origin, combining it with Emilian influences in order to produce a painting which displays great formal balance and notable expository clarity.

After the deaths of Giulio Cesare Procaccini in 1626, Morazzone in 1626, Daniele Crespi in 1630 and Cerano in 1632 and the crisis caused by the plague epidemic of 1630, a new phase started in Lombard painting with the opening to the Roman and Genoese Baroque movements and through the revaluation of

the Venetian painting of the Cinquecento. The main participants in the new developments were Francesco Cairo, who worked in Milan and Turin, Giovan Battista Discepoli from Lugano and the brothers Carlo Francesco and Giuseppe Nuvolone, so well as a number of minor artists.

The *Agony in the Garden* by Cairo is a theme that the artist was extremely fond of in his early period, when he was very much influenced by Morazzone and was also in contact with Giulio Cesare Procaccini and Tanzio da Varallo, from whom he derived his Caravaggesque element, while the stylistic feature which is so typical of the painter is the metallic quality of the light in the general obscurity. The small *Saint Catherine in Ecstasy* can be dated after his educational journey to Rome, with the enrichment which resulted from his encounter with the Cortonesque Baroque, and after close contact with Van Dyck and the Genoese school. The *Portrait of Luigi Scaramuccia*, which in the past was erroneously believed to depict Fulvio Testi, also belongs to this period. Besides its artistic merits this painting was important from a historical point of view because it portrays the famous man of letters and painter, the author of *Finezze de' pennelli italiani* to which the initials F. P. on the book in the foreground allude. Scaramuccia brought Reni's classicism to the artistic milieu of Milan, where he arrived in 1657. The painting is, therefore, "symbolic homage to a connoisseur of painting and of the Milanese artistic milieu, which had been dominated by Cairo until his death in 1665" (Porzio, in *Pinacoteca di Brera...*, 1989, p. 185).

Signed and dated 1646, the *Assumption of the Virgin* by Carlo Francesco Nuvolone, formerly in the church of Santa Maria del Lentasio in Milan is one of the painter's most significant works, together with two altarpieces, the *Purification* (1645) in Piacenza and the *Virgin with Saint Charles Borromeo and Saint Felix of Cantalice* in Parma (1647). Thanks to the stimulus provided by Pietro da Cortona and the Genoese and Emilian

41

Cerano, Morazzone, Giulio Cesare Procaccini,
Martyrdom of Saint Rufina and Saint Seconda.

Camillo Procaccini, Adoration of the Shepherds.

Tanzio da Varallo, Martyrdom of the Franciscans in Nagasaki.

schools, his decidedly Baroque orientation, both as regards composition and the handling of the paint, went beyond the limits of early seventeenth century Lombard Mannerism within which Nuvolone had confined himself in his more youthful works. An important source of inspiration has been identified as the *Assumption of the Virgin* by Guido Reni in the church of the Jesuits of Sant'Ambrogio in Genoa.

Very few examples survive of Nuvolone's output of portraits, which was extolled by contemporary sources, who especially mention a portrait of the Archduchess Anne of Austria that was painted in 1640 when she visited Lombardy. Among those that still exist is the *Family of the Artist*, a group portrait in which, together with Carlo Franceso are depicted his brother Giuseppe playing the lute, his wife playing the harp and, in the background, his father Panfilo.

The contribution of Genoese painting with its vivid colours and the all-pervading vigour of Baroque is evident both in the *Temptation of Saint Anthony Abbot* by Giovan Battista Discepoli called Zoppo da Lugano, from the church of San Carpoforo in Milan, and also in the *Flagellation* by Giuseppe Nuvolone, part of a cycle in the Sala dei Senatori in the Ducal Palace in Milan. In both cases the contribution was enriched by a fresh interpretation of the local pictorial tradition, now seen with a new sensibility.

The straightforward representation of the natural world which was so typical of the Bergamasque and Brescian schools over the centuries was confirmed in the Seicento by the austere naturalism of the portraiture of Carlo Ceresa, whose *Portrait of a Lady of the Sola Family* is in the Brera, and by the output of still lifes by Evaristo Baschenis, which centred on the themes of *Musical Instruments* and *Kitchen Scenes*, present in the Brera with two splendid paintings which have played a decisive role in the revaluation of the artist by modern critics.

The poor opinion which until recently critics had of Lombard painting in the Settecento —

44

Francesco Cairo, Portrait of Luigi Scaramuccia.
Carlo Ceresa, Portrait of a Lady of the Sola
Family.

with the exception of the naturalistic current (portraits, still lifes and genre scenes), which for some time has been the subject of serious studies—has had negative repercussions on the size of the collection of these works in the gallery.

The large religious paintings by Abbiati, Legnanino, Lanzani and Magatti, which came to Brera from the suppressed churches, have nearly all been sent outside the gallery for storage, so that many of them run serious risk of damage or loss, despite the fact that they may be of considerable importance. For example the *Nativity* and the *Appearance of Christ to Saint Jerome* by Legnanino, key works of the painter's mature period, are now at the church of San Marco in Milan, while the superb *Death of Saint Joseph* by Magatti is stored at Ossona. Nevertheless medium-sized and small works have remained in the Brera, and among them is a series of self-portraits by artists in the "Gallery of Portraits of Painters" set up by Giuseppe Bossi following the example of other famous single-theme collections, such as the Florentine one in the Uffizi.

Painting in Milan in the late seventeenth and early eighteenth centuries, at the moment of the transition from High Baroque to Late Baroque is represented by the self-portraits of Lanzani, a leading follower of the Marattesque current, and by Legnanino, who was perhaps the most advanced of the painters of his generation owing to his synthesis of the various contributions of Emilian academicism, Roman classicism and Baroque and Genoese grand decorative painting.

The complex cultural web of the period is reflected in the interesting *Martyrdom of Saint Erasmus* which has been attributed to both Magnasco and Abbiati and, recently to Sebastiano Ricci (M. Olivari, in *Pinacoteca...*, 1990, pp. 212-213).

The latter's relations with Magnasco, who in his turn was a pupil of Abbiati, were maintained both in Ricci's Milanese period and also in Florence and Venice. The cycle of four *Landscapes* by Magnasco, from the church of

Stefano Maria Legnani called il Legnanino,
Self-portrait.

Santa Maria delle Grazie at Gravedona (although they were originally painted for the house of a noble family on Lake Como), was inopportunely split up between the gallery and the Italian Embassy in London. However, illustration of the artist's grotesquely surreal genre is provided from his early output by two *Ruins*, executed in collaboration with the Milanese Clemente Spera, who painted the backgrounds of architecture, following a procedure that was customary at the time and which Magnasco only abandoned in his mature period.

Carlo Innocenzo Carloni, one of the protagonists on a European level of Rococo grand decoration, is represented by a preparatory sketch for the frescoes in Asti Cathedral, the *Triumph of the Faith*. Another drawing, the *Aurora* by Gaetano Trabellesi, which was a preparatory sketch for a ceiling in the Palazzo Reale in Milan, is an indication, little more than a decade later, of the birth of the Neoclassical style, whose followers in Milan included Albertolli, Piermarini, Trabellesi and Martino Knoller, all artists who were to a greater or lesser extent linked to the Fine Arts Academy founded by Maria Theresa in the building of the former College of the Jesuits in Brera.

The naturalistic current of the "painters of reality," which thrived above all in Venetian Lombardy (in other words the areas round Bergamo and Brescia), is well represented in the gallery, partly due to recent purchases. The Bergamasque Ghislandi, who had learned his craft in Venice with Sebastiano Bombelli, in his portraits merged the Venetian and Lombard traditions, combining the splendid colours of the lacquers with a sober rendering of the natural world which recalls Ceresa and, in the more distant past, Cavagna, Moroni and Moretto. Giacomo Ceruti was born in Milan, but trained in Brescia where his cultural background was formed. The *Porters*, reunited in the Brera thanks to two separate gifts, are generally identified by scholars as those referred to in the eighteenth century by Carboni in the "quinta

camera" of Casa Barbisoni in Brescia. They relate to the theme of pauperism which the painter was encouraged to take up by a number of enlightened members of the Brescian nobility and clergy. The two *Still Lifes*, formerly in the collection of Abbot Carlo Bianconi, the first secretary of the Brera Academy, must have been painted in Ceruti's last years in Milan. They are remarkable for "an attention to the light that is almost Neo-Caravaggesque" and for "a revival of the skilful use of colour in Baschenis's kitchen scenes" (Morandotti in *Pinacoteca di Brera...*, 1989, p. 127). Francesco Londonio is directly linked to the calmer atmosphere of Ceruti's genre painting in his late Milanese period. Indeed, Londonio's pastoral themes, fostered by memories of the Bamboccianti and the Italo-Flemish animalists, may be directly placed in the period of transition from Arcadia to Enlightenment.

The Venetian School
Mariolina Olivari

The collection of Venetian paintings in the Brera is the most important one, both in terms of quantity and quality, that exists outside Venice. This state of affairs is obviously the result of the factors that led to the birth and development of the gallery's collection in the nineteenth century. Following the dissolution of the religious orders numerous works of art poured into Milan from Venice and its mainland territories.

In accordance with the canons of taste of the times, in the selection of the works to be displayed preference was invariably given to those of the Quattrocento and Cinquecento, while the majority of the Seicento works were dispatched to storerooms outside the gallery or bartered with antique dealers and collectors. The same fate awaited the Settecento paintings, which in any case were not present in large quantities, with the exception of a number of very large paintings, such as the *Transport of the Holy Ark* by Sebastiano Ricci or the painting of the same subject by Angelo Trevisani. Formerly in the Venetian church of Santi Cosma e Damiano at the Giudecca, these works were originally sent to the Louvre, then they came to Milan, from where they were sent in 1818 to Somaglia Lodigiana, where they are still in storage.

The Trecento is represented by the polyptych by Lorenzo Veneziano depicting the *Virgin and Child Enthroned with Eight Saints* from Santa Maria della Celestia. Originally put up for sale and then sent to the Academy of Vienna, the work returned to Italy after the First World War. It came to the Brera in 1950 in exchange for the *Coronation of the Virgin* by Paolo Veneziano, which was then sent to the Gallerie dell'Accademia in Venice in order to reunite it with the other panels of the polyptych from which it originally came, since these had remained in Venice at the time of the dissolution of the religious orders. Elegant and still decidedly Byzantinesque, the refined altarpiece is a product of the last years of the artist, who is documented as being active until 1372.

The lively and resolute stylistic features displayed by the Master of the Pesaro Crucifix in a small panel painting, the *Virgin and Child and Annunciation* can be linked to the Gothic style influenced by the Bolognese school of Lorenzo. The initials *TS* interwoven in a monogram, which is repeated a number of times in the background, indicate that it was probably commissioned by the Venetian guild of the Tessitori di Seta (silk weavers). It is by artist who must have been active in Venice towards the end of the century and who was influenced not only by Lorenzo, but also by the arrival in the city of Giovanni da Bologna and the archaic style of Nicolò di Pietro.

The *Coronation of the Virgin* by the latter artist, who brings us to the beginning of the Quattrocento, repeats an iconography that is characteristic of the painter and which is repeated almost identically in the paintings of the same subject in the Accademia dei Concordi in Rovigo and the Galleria Nazionale in Rome. The refinement of the frame, which is both original and complete, is echoed by the enamelled and compressed surfaces of the panel, where are very much in evidence the small figures of the family of donors kneeling at the base of the double throne on which are seated the Virgin and Christ, who is placing a crown on her head.

The elegance and naturalistic approach of the Late Gothic period, which was predicted by the grace of the previous paintings, finds complete and very refined expression in the *Adoration of the Magi*, signed by Stefano da Verona and dated 1435 (but the last figure, retouched in modern times, was interpreted in the past also as 4 or 6). Above the meticulously painted small plants of violets and carnations, which are symbols of Christ's humanity and passion, assembles a large group of slender personages who are delineated with a refined sense of fluidity. Refined too are the great number of details that enrich the composition, in which there is abundant evidence of influence by Pisanello and Gentile da Fabriano. The courtly style of the Veronese artist, who died shortly afterwards (in fact his activity is documented only until

1438) is the last expression of International
Gothic. With the *Virgin and Child* by Jacopo
Bellini, dated 1448, as the vigorous and syn-
thesized composition of the figures shows, we
have definitely entered the Renaissance.

Also the *Praglia Polyptych* by Giovanni
d'Alemagna and Antonio Vivarini was probably executed in 1448. Its name derived from
the place of origin, near Padua. The donor
kneeling below the Virgin has been identified
as Cipriano Rinaldini, an important abbot of
the Paduan Benedictines who is thought to
have commissioned the work in order to celebrate the union of the abbey with the Congre-
gation of Saint Justina. The fact that the polyptych was painted by two artists, although
it has been challenged by some critics (Pallucchini, Mariani Canova) is now incontest-
able, but precisely which of the panels should
be attributed to each of the two artists is still
open to debate. In any case both were linked
to an archaic taste that was not devoid of By-
zantinism, which was typical of the Muranese
school of which Antonio was one of the most
important followers.

Stylistic affinities with Paduan and Squarcionesque schools characterised the works of the
Venetian Carlo Crivelli, who was documented in 1468 in Zara (now Zadar) in Dalmatia
and then lived for a large part of his life in the
Marches. In the *Camerino Triptych* (1482),
from the church of San Domenico in Camerino in the Marches (Zampetti, 1986), his
taut wiry style, enriched with refinements
that are still apparently Late Gothic in character (the gold backgrounds, details ren-
dered in an illusionistic manner in relief with
the technique of raised gesso, the presence of
large quantities of fruit and flowers which are
Marian and Christological symbols) reveals
features in common with Mantegna and it
adopts a manner that is, at least in part, anti-
thetic to the wholly Renaissance style of Bellini. Also from Camerino, but in this case
from the Cathedral of Santa Maria Maggiore,
comes the fascinating *Madonna della Candeletta*, the central panel of a polyptych that
was dismantled after the earthquake which

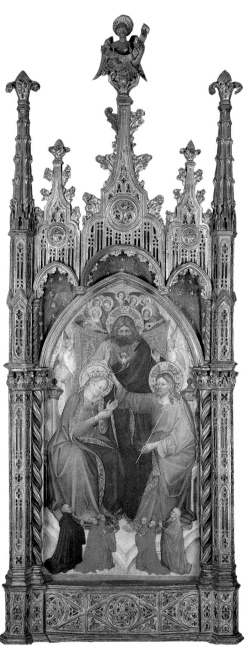

hit the city in 1799 and was then dispersed by the dissolution of the religious orders to various places. Commissioned from the artist in 1488, the polyptych was most probably completed some years later, around 1490-91. According to the proposal for reconstruction put forward by Zampetti (1961), the cymatium of the large polyptych was another panel painting in the Brera, the *Crucifixion with Saint John and the Virgin*, which fascinatingly is an expression of the consonance between the austere faces of the personages and the metallic harshness of the draperies and their flowing locks.

However, in the *Madonna della Candeletta* the decorative element prevails. The rich damask fabrics, the luxuriant festoons of fruit and leaves, the highly skilled and very meticulous rendering of the materials are a demonstration of the painter's keen sense of form towards the end of his career. Lastly the *Coronation of the Virgin with the Trinity and Saint Venanzio, Saint John the Baptist, Saint Catherine of Alexandria, Saint Augustine (?), Saint Francis and Saint Sebastian* was painted in 1493. It was originally surmounted by a lunette depicting the *Pietà*, which is considered to be one of the artist's masterpieces. It took Crivelli three years to execute the work for the church of San Francesco at Fabriano (in fact the original contract is dated 1490), making use of an iconography that complied strictly with Franciscan precepts. The brilliance of the enamelled surfaces is softened by reddish-pink glazes which are spread over the rich decorative sections. Filling the space to an almost unbelievable extent, but nevertheless concealing it without eliminating it, this magnificent display remains as one of the fundamental works for the interpretation of the extraordinary phantasmagorical Renaissance of the Venetian artist.

The comparison between the Crivelli panels and the *Saint Luke Polyptych* by Andrea Mantegna, executed between 1453 and 1454, immediately emphasizes the extent to which the artist was more advanced. The adoption

Andrea Mantegna, Dead Christ. ✓

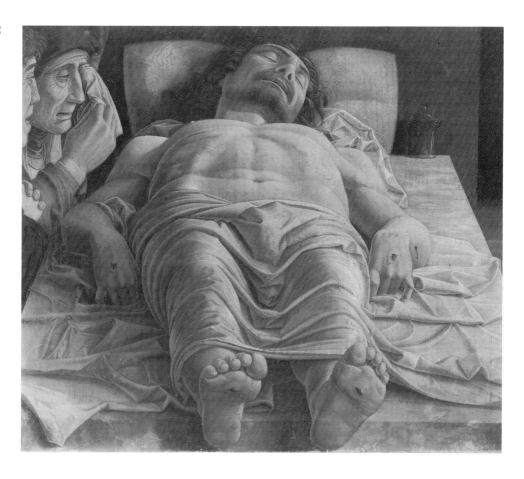

of the traditional composition of the polyptych on two levels, with the saints disposed symmetrically on the sides of the principal panel, over which a representation of the Pietà juts out, is brought alive in the case of Mantegna not only with a very strong line, the fruit of his training with his master Francesco Squarcione, but also by a compact plasticity of the perspective, which reveals the influence of Donatello's sojourn in Padua and of the great Florentine sculptor's high altar in the church of Sant'Antonio.

Mantegna was also responsible for the *Dead Christ*, which has always been considered to be one of his greatest masterpieces. Listed among the painter's possessions at the time of his death, the tempera painting on canvas was sold by his heirs to the Gonzaga family. It disappeared without trace until the beginning of the nineteenth century, when it was purchased by the gallery from heirs of Giuseppe Bossi, the first secretary of the Brera. Conceived as a lamentation, which justifies from an iconographic point of view the presence of three mourners on the left, the painting becomes, in its austere, essential composure, one of the dramatic high points of the Quattrocento. A strongly incised line indicates the faces and stresses with tragic harshness Christ's wounds and the sorrowful grimaces of Saint John and the Virgin, while the sharp foreshortening of Christ's body makes it more convincing and striking.

Formerly attributed to Giovanni Bellini, who was Mantegna's brother-in-law and his partner in an intense artistic relationship, the *Virgin and Child with Cherubs*, probably executed around 1485, brings to a close the series of works wholly by the artist's hand present in the Brera collections.

In fact, the subject-matter and the forms that are softer than previously cause it to be closer to analogous works by Giovanni Bellini. The *Virgin and Child*, also known as the *Madonna Greca* because of the presence of an inscription in Greek at the top of the painting, was an early work by the latter artist. The smooth, harmonious forms and gentle immobility remind us of the Byzantine origins of this type of image. On the other hand his mature *Virgin and Child*, dated 1510, in which the fusion between figures and landscape has now taken place and the diffusion of lyricism that is delicate, ineffable, but very intense brings to mind the new tonal approach of Giorgione.

Not long after the *Madonna Greca*, in other words around 1470, another masterpiece by Giovanni Bellini must have been painted. this was the *Pietà*, donated to the Brera by Hortense de Eugène de Beauharnais in 1811. The sense of intimate, harrowing drama is echoed by the silent deserted landscape and the empty metallic sky behind the figures. The line is gouged out, still reflecting the influence of Donatello and Mantegna, engraving with painful precision the interlaced hands of the mother and dead son and the drawing together of their emaciated faces. At the base of the tomb an inscription adapted from a verse of the *Elegies* by Propertius stresses the emotional involvement of the artist in the tragic event, which he interprets from the viewpoint of his humanistic cultural background.

The result of the collaboration of the two Bellini brothers, Gentile and Giovanni, the huge painting of *Saint Mark Preaching at Alexandria* originally hung in the Scuola di San Marco in Venice. (The "Scuole" of Venice were confraternities dedicated to good works.)

How much each of the two artists contributed is still a matter for debate, but it is generally agreed that Gentile, who had begun the work in 1504, was responsible for the overall composition. However Giovanni, who following a request in his brother's will had agreed to complete it after Gentile's death in 1507, can be credited with the greater modernity and dynamism which can be observed in the work if it is compared with its pendant, the *Procession of the Relic of the True Cross* (now in the Gallerie dell'Accademia in Venice). The exotic architecture in the background, which feels the effects of the Turkish culture that Gentile had absorbed during his sojourn at

*Giovanni and Gentile Bellini, Saint Mark
Preaching at Alexandria.*

*Vittore Carpaccio, The Dispute of Saint Stephen
(after restoration).*

the court of the Sultan in Constantinople, is echoed in the foreground by the orderly disposition of the figures, which are brought to life by keenly-observed individual portraits. The great long-lived figure of Giovanni Bellini was that of a charismatic patriarch who dominated Venetian painting from the Quattrocento to the early Cinquecento. Artists who were quite different from him felt his influence; this was the case of Vittorio Carpaccio, a fascinating narrator of stories which were a subtle mixture of fantasy and visual precision. The two *Stories of the Virgin*, the *Presentation at the Temple* and the *Betrothal*, which are part of a dispersed cycle of six paintings which originally adorned the Scuola degli Albanesi in Venice, were executed in the first decade of the Cinquecento. In these works, and in the later and more remarkable *Disputation of Saint Stephen*, which comes from the cycle in the Scuola di Santo Stefano in Venice, Carpaccio reveals with great inventiveness his distinctive aesthetic ideals in which the intensity of colour and the orderly dimensions of a perfect spatial setting merge in a complex style that evokes memories of the Flemish painters as well as Antonello da Messina.

Also Giovanni Battista Cima da Conegliano, who painted numerous works which are now in the Brera (at least eight are ascribed to the artist and three to his workshop), after being influenced by Alvise Vivarini in his early period, was attracted, especially during the last decade of the Quattrocento, by the work of Giovanni Bellini. His calm and harmonious painting, distinguished by the solidity of the compositions and the bright, warm colours, is perfectly illustrated by the three large altarpieces depicting the *Virgin and Child Enthroned with Four Saints and Members of a Confraternity* (c. 1488), *Saint Peter Martyr, Saint Nicholas and Saint Benedict* (1505-06) and *Saint Peter Enthroned with Saint John the Baptist and Saint Paul* (1516), which is the last of his documented works. In fact, he died a year later in his native town of Conegliano.

Lorenzo Lotto, Febo from Brescia.
Paris Bordon, Two Lovers.

Bartolomeo Montagna, an artist from Vicenza, combined typically Venetian stylistic attributes of Giovanni Battista with Lombard influences drawn, above all, from Bramante and the sculpture of Giovanni Antonio Amadeo and Cristoforo and Antonio Mantegazza, which he had perhaps seen during a journey to the Certosa di Pavia, for which he had painted a large altarpiece in 1490. The complex perspective framework of the *Virgin and Child Enthroned with Saint Monica, Saint Andrew, Saint Ursula and Saint Sigismund*, executed between 1496 and 1500 for Bartolomeo Quarzi, stresses the relationship between the figures and the architecture, recalling analogous works by Bernardo Zenale. Liberale da Verona, a miniaturist and painter, executed the panel painting depicting *Saint Sebastian*, probably between 1490 and 1500, for the church of San Domenico in Ancona. Against a crowded background, notable for the extreme foreshortening, stands the dominant figure of the Saint, which is evidently derived from the statue of Adam executed by Antonio Rizzo for the Doge's Palace in Venice. As a result of his sojourn in Tuscany, where he worked as a miniaturist, Liberale added the influence of the Umbrian and Tuscan artists to the Late Gothic expressionism of his early period, but his line was now tauter, having become angular and incisive, thanks to models of Mantegnesque derivation.

The style displayed by the little-known Michele da Verona is simpler and more linear in the most important and complex work of his in the gallery. This is the enormous *Crucifixion* dated 1501, which was formerly in the refectory of the monastery of San Giorgio in Braida in Verona, which was completely rebuilt by the canons regular of San Lorenzo Giustiniani between 1447 and 1518. This rebuilding was what brought about the commission for the huge canvas, which was almost unknown until the last century, when the monastery was suppressed. The artist was almost certainly inspired by another work that has now been lost: the fresco of the same subject executed by Jacopo Bellini for Verona Cathedral. Paying no attention to Mantegna, Michele seems rather to have been influenced by Domenico and Francesco Morone, important figures in Veronese art in the late Quattrocento and early Cinquecento.

The *Virgin and Child with Saint Zeno and Saint Nicholas* which Francesco Morone painted a year after Michele's *Crucifixion* was executed, that is to say in 1502, appears in its austere and ornate elegance to have been influenced by Mantegna, especially as regards the decorative elements, while the solid forms of the figures seem to have stylistic affinities with Antonello.

The heyday of the Venetian Cinquecento is represented in the Brera by a number of undisputed masterpieces. For example, the courtly *Portrait of Antonio Porcia* by Titian is accompanied by the vibrant light of the panel painting depicting *Saint Jerome in Penitence* which the artist painted around 1555. By exploiting the limited tonality of the priming as if it were true paint, Titian created an extremely rich variety of effects in the *Saint Jerome*, where light and shade intertwine and expand, assuming an emotional and evocative role which has great visual power.

Lotto was a restless artist, who is often inappropriately contrasted with the all-powerful Titian. Besides a number of religious paintings, Brera boasts four portraits by the painter which fully reveal his keenly sensitive humanity. The couple constituted by *Laura da Pola* and *Febo da Brescia* and the other two, the *Old Man with Gloves* and the *Portrait of a Gentleman*, all unforgettable and very immediate interlocutors with the observer, are among the soberest and most convincing portraits of the Cinquecento.

In the same period Paris Bordon, who came from Treviso, with his *Two Lovers* produced a brilliant example of his totally different approach to the portrait. The sitters, whom the decidedly Giorgionesque stylistic choices of the artist subjects to the suffused languor of tonality, are sensual, subtly allusive figures that are kept at a distance in a refined, intellectualistic world.

Among the important collection of works by Jacopo Tintoretto in the gallery is conspicuous the *Finding of the Body of Saint Mark*, which with another two paintings depicting stories from the life of the saint, adorned the Scuola Grande di San Marco in Venice. Commissioned by the Guardian of the Scuola, Tommaso Rangone, who is depicted kneeling in the centre of the painting in the robes of the office of "golden knight," the cycle was commenced by Tintoretto in 1548. The painting in the Brera was executed between 1562 an 1566 and marks a high point in the artist's career. Majestically visionary, composed on a finely balanced perspective axis that gives the space a sense of dramatic dynamism, this work produces with the unreal light—which only partially coagulates to illuminate the architecture and draperies—an extraordinarily expressive means. The lunette depicting the *Pietà* which dates to 1563 and the altarpiece with *Saint Helena, Saint Barbara, Saint Andrew, Saint Macarius, Another Saint and a Donor* (c. 1506), more conventional and mannered, display the typical features of the painter's output that were to become models from which succeeding generations would seek inspiration.

Another great artist of the second half of the Cinquecento in Venice, Paolo Caliari called Veronese, painted the *Feast in the House of Simon*, which the gallery obtained in exchange for the *Feast of Saint Gregory*, which in 1817 was returned to the Santuario di Monte Berico in Vicenza, from where it had originally come. Painted in 1570 for the refectory of the monastery of San Sebastiano in Venice, the painting forms part of the series of Veronese's sumptuous feast scenes which led to the artist being tried for heresy, but it is one of the less striking and structurally simpler examples. In fact, among the works in the Brera other smaller paintings by Veronese appear to be better illustrations of the artist's skill, such as the *Baptism and Temptation of Christ*, a freshly creative work, in

Jacopo Tintoretto, *Finding of the Body of Saint Mark.*

Paolo Veronese, Baptism and Temptation of Christ.

which invention and sensibility to colour are firmly wedded, and the intense *Agony in the Garden*, where the pinks and purplish-blues that emerge from the nocturnal background are brilliantly handled.

The Bassano family's flourishing and prolific workshop is represented by an important work by its founder, Jacopo. This is the altarpiece which depicts *Saint Roch Healing the Plague-stricken*, executed by the artist for the church of San Rocco in Vicenza, perhaps after the plague epidemic of 1575. The realistic portrayal of the sick to whom the Saint is ministering decidely contrast with the more conventional figure of the interceding Virgin above, which is believed by some scholars to have been painted by Jacopo's eldest son, Francesco.

Besides the great Venetian painters, the schools of the Venetian mainland territories in Lombardy are present with a number of important works by their principal followers. In Brescia naturalism, austere and balanced in the case of Moretto (*Gardone Polyptych and Virgin and Child*) and sanguine and northern in the case of Romanino (*Presentation of Christ at the Temple and Virgin and Child*), accompanies the enormous panel painting depicting the *Virgin and Child in Glory with Saint Peter, Saint Jerome and Saint Dominic* by Giovanni Gerolamo Savoldo. Considered one of the masterpieces of this artist, who had only a very limited output, it was executed in 1524-25 for the Dominicans in Pesaro. The complex and still enigmatic cultural background of the artist can be sensed in this work, with its magnificent composition that is, however, amazingly simple, where the four figures of the saints stand out with monumental emphasis against a vast expanse of landscape. The illusory transparency of the light, for which the painter was famed, is diffused in the limpid air, revealing the volumes of the bodies and draperies. Savoldo, who at that time was resident in Venice, would certainly have been aware both of the work that Titian was producing, and also the original output, which was not always understood, of Lorenzo Lotto, who had then returned to his native city after his long stay in Bergamo.

Shortly after the beginning of the century in Bergamo the influence of Milanese art was increasingly being replaced by ideas imported from Venice, not only by Lotto, but also by the descendants of Giovanni Cariani, Andrea

60

Previtali and Palma Vecchio. From Bergamo come the brilliant *Virgin and Child Enthroned with Saints* by Cariani, the very limpid *Transfiguration* by Previtali, whose iconographic characteristics have sometimes caused it to be interpreted as a *Baptism of Christ*, and the Olympian panels from a polyptych depicting *Saint Helena and Constantine*, *Saint Roch* and *Saint Sebastian* (which may come from Val Imagna near Bergamo) by Palma Vecchio.

In the second half of the century Giovan Battista Moroni assumed a position of great prominence. While his altarpieces (*Assumption of the Virgin* and *Virgin and Child with Saints*) are characterised by the evident influence of Moretto (in fact he had been the pupil of the Brescian artist), his portraits— among which is particularly noteworthy the one of *Antonio Navagero* (1565), the masterpiece of his "red" period—lucidly reflect the real world in a way that has earned the artist the right to be considered the initiator of the so-called painting of reality.

The Brera possesses a number of outstanding works from the festive and complex period of the Venetian Seicento. However, many of these are very large and unfortunately this has, in the majority of cases, caused them to be placed in churches or other buildings far from the gallery, where it is difficult for the public to see them. Nevertheless some works have recently been brought back to the gallery, thus permitting at least two of these magnificent works to be admired: the *Victory of the Inhabitants of Chartres over the Normans* by Alessandro Varotari, called Padovanino, and the *Fall of the Rebel Angels* by Francesco Maffei from Vicenza. The former work, dated 1618, comes from the church of Santa Maria Maggiore in Venice, where it was part of a rich decorative display which included another five paintings by the Paduan artist. It illustrates the miraculous victory of the inhabitants of Chartres over their besiegers by displaying the Virgin's veil. Considered one of the most important followers of the traditionalist school, Varotari pro-

duces here a work which is characterised by bland classicism of Titianesque and Romanist derivation, with composed, carefully controlled dynamism.

The large painting by Maffei, an imaginative and refined genius, is dated 1656. It was originally in the church of San Michele in Vicenza, where it was the pendant of a second large work with the same format, the *Last Judgement* by Giulio Carpioni, which was executed a year later (also belonging to the Brera, this work is at present in the Episcopal Seminary at Venegono Inferiore, near Varese, where the painting by Maffei was for a long period). Pervaded by an unsteady, diaphanous bluish-pink light, the maelstrom of angels darkens as it descends, indicating the fall and condemnation of the rebels. The spiralling foreshortened perspectives, the impetuous entangling of limbs and draperies, stressed by spectacular explosions of red and blue and the extremely dynamic way the paint is handled, are wholly Baroque, while the bright, transparent union of light and colour is a precursor of Settecento luminosity.

The lively, varied pictorial culture of Sebastiano Ricci, who came from Belluno, was of fundamental importance for the renewal of Venetian art in the late Seicento and early Settecento. It was the result not only of the versatile nature of his talent, but also of the his eventful life, during which he went to Venice, Parma, Florence, Rome, Milan and Vienna and then to England, to mention just a few of the most important places he visited. Right from the early nineteenth century lack of space caused an enormous painting (450 x 800 cm) by Ricci to be sent to the parish church of Somaglia Lodigiana. Depicting the *Transport of the Holy Ark* and dated 1729, it is a splendid example of the artist's decorative virtuosity, which so influenced Piazzetta, Pellegrini, Gianantonio and Francesco Guardi and Giandomenico Tiepolo. The small altarpiece depicting *Saint Gaetano Ministering to a Dying Man* from a subsidiary chapel in the Cathedral in Bergamo, a city where Ricci frequently worked, indi-

Giambattista Tiepolo, The Temptation of Saint Anthony.

cates that this is a special moment in the artist's career, characterised by a fluid brushstroke and soft, oblique luminarism. The unusual, bloodcurdling *Martyrdom of Saint Erasmus*, on the other hand, is evidence of the close, problematic relationship between Ricci and one of the most brilliant and complex figures of north Italian art, Alessandro Magnasco.

Heir to the great Venetian decorative tradition of the Cinquecento and Seicento, Giambattista Tiepolo in the *Madonna del Carmelo with Saint Simon Stock, Saint Teresa of Avila, Saint Alberto da Vercelli and the Prophet Elijah*, executed between 1721 and 1727, produced one of the most delightful works of his early period. Devised to be viewed from the

side, (in fact, it was originally on the right wall of a side chapel in Sant'Aponal in Venice) the composition of the painting is very unusual, with all the main figures gathered on one side. With their forms sculptured by the chiaroscuro, they evidently feel the influence of tenebrism and Piazzetta, but the artist's vast pictorial culture is made evident by references to Veronese, Titian and Solimena. Another early work by the artist is the small painting depicting the *Temptation of Saint Anthony*. Abounding in delicate contrasts of light and colour, which range from pearly pink to warm smoky greys, it must have been painted around 1725, when themes relating to the friaries were in vogue. After some uncertainty whether they should be attributed

Giovan Battista Piazzetta, Rebecca at the Well.

Francesco Guardi, Grand Canal with the Fabbriche Nuove at the Rialto, (after restoration).

to Giambattista Tiepolo or his son Giandomenico, it seems to be generally agreed that the latter was responsible for the painted sketch depicting *Saint Faustino and Saint Giovita Appearing in Defence of Brescia*, with its vigorous, rapid handling and the sensuous, delicate *Saint Luigi Gonzaga*, depicted half-length on an oval canvas.

A few years older than Giambattista Tiepolo, whom he greatly influenced, was Giovanni Battista Piazzetta. The Brera boasts one of his most famous works, *Rebecca at the Well*, which was probably executed between 1735 and 1740 for Alvise Contarini. The work was reproduced as an engraving in 1740 by Pietro Monaco together with its pendant depicting *Judith and Holofernes* (this work is now in a private collection). The biblical theme is interpreted with the freshness and elegance of an Arcadian idyll. Here too the large number of stylistic affinities, which range from Rubens to the French painters, bear witness to the European character of Venetian Rococo. But Piazzetta's origins, which went back to the Caravaggesque style as interpreted by Giovanni Battista Crespi and the Venetian *tenebrosi*, are revealed in the uniquely soft and intense impasto obtained by means of chiaroscuro, which in the period when *Rebecca* was painted attained its most luminous effects.

Another European protagonist of history painting in the first half of the century was Giovanni Battista Pittoni. His style was heavily influenced by Ricci and had contacts with Antonio Balestra, Nicolò Grassi and Federico Bencovich. *Hannibal Swearing Vengeance on the Romans*, executed after 1720, repeats a theme which the artist had already dealt with in a series of small paintings that were evidently intended for private collectors and are now dispersed among various museums and collections. As in the later *Bacchus and Ariadne*, the surfaces are defined in the light and form by a continuously varying contrast of vigorous and graceful use of colour.

Side by side with history painting, the Venetian *veduta* painting genre established itself as a very successful phenomenon in Settecento art. Producing paintings that were frequently true masterpieces, Antonio Canal called Canaletto and his nephew, Bernardo Bellotto, excelled in their unrivalled ability to reproduce light and the transparency of the air. Canaletto painted the *Quay of the Bacino di San Marco* and the *Grand Canal from Campo San Vio*, portraying an immortal Venice that is glorified in the perfection of its serenity. His nephew Bellotto painted the two unusual *Views of Gazzada*, a village near Varese. They are the fruit of the journey which the artist made to Lombardy as a young man in 1744, shortly before he left Italy in order to work in Saxony, Austria, Bavaria and Poland. Considered the masterpieces of Bellotto's Italian period, the two views constitute a totally new approach, both because of the emotional involvement which is matched by the lucidity of his vision and also because the painter had for the first time, in the painting depicting Villa Melzi, given a precise temporal context to the light by choosing to bathe the view in the sharp, pure dawn air.

In complete contrast to Canaletto's brilliantly illuminated Venice, the disquieting, secretly dramatic interpretation of the city by Francesco Guardi, is revealed to us in the *Grand Canal towards the Rialto with the Palazzo Grimani and the Palazzo Manin* and its pendant the *Grand Canal with the Fabbriche Nuove at the Rialto*, which may be dated around 1755. Only the expansion of pictorial space based on a wide panoramic view and the predominance of a sunny bluish tone remind us of the stylistic affinities with Canaletto which were the basis of the view painting of Guardi, who was the last creative — and in his own manner pre-Romantic — practitioner of the *veduta* genre.

The Schools of Emilia-Romagna and Central and Southern Italy

Enrico Noè

The schools of painting of Emilia, Romagna and Central and Southern Italy are not uniformly represented in the Brera Gallery. In fact, while there is a continuous record of the history of painters from Emilia-Romagna from the fourteenth to the eighteenth centuries, Tuscan, Roman and Neapolitan artists are definitely rather thin on the ground. This scarcity is explained, to a large extent, by the way the gallery was initiated, linked as it was to the Napoleonic Italian state, of which it was intended to be the artistic synthesis. Consequently the Brera possesses a large number of works from the territories which between 1805 and 1814 formed part of the Italian Kingdom, which as far as the scope of this chapter is concerned included central and eastern Emilia (excluding, that is, Piacenza and Parma) and the Marches. Paintings from other regions of Central and Southern Italy only came to the gallery fortuitously and sporadically as a result of purchases after the end of the Napoleonic era.

A part of a panel from a polyptych, depicting *Saint Laurence*, by Bernardo Daddi (c. 1290-1348?) is a direct, albeit limited, testimony to the level reached by the art of the Florentine Trecento after Giotto. A great Sienese who was strongly influenced by Giotto, Ambrogio Lorenzetti (c. 1280-1348?), painted a *Virgin and Child* (donated in 1947), which can be dated about 1340, that is to say in the period immediately after the famous frescoes in the Palazzo Pubblico in Siena (1337-39). In the expressions of the mother and child it is possible to distinguish new psychological animation, which is the direct result of those revolutionary works.

Still by a Sienese artist, but towards the beginning of the Quattrocento, there is the polyptych depicting the *Coronation of the Virgin with Four Saints*, by Andrea di Bartolo (c. 1370-1428). From Sant'Angelo in Vado, near Urbino, it is a significant example of Sienese artistic taste in the late Trecento, which was so firmly linked to the style of Simone Martini, as can be seen by the softness of the lines and the brilliant colours of the forms.

The Riminese school is represented by three small panels depicting *Stories from the Life of Saint Columba*, which certainly belonged to a dismembered polyptych (donated in 1960). The work is attributed to an anonymous artist, who is in fact known as the Master of Saint Columba, and more recently to Giovanni Baronzio (active in the first half of the Trecento). The Riminese school, which derived directly from Giotto was a brief phenomenon, which only lasted until about 1360, but was very intense, as is clearly demonstrated by the efficacious, fluent narrative of these small panels, which are sustained by an architectural perspective that is still empirical and charmingly inconsistent.

The Marches gave birth to an important protagonist of the following period, known as International Gothic: this was Gentile da Fabriano (c. 1370-1427), who, however, worked over a large area including Venice, Florence and Rome, where he diffused a delicate, fantastic Gothic style. His great ability can already be perceived in the early *Polyptych* from Valle Romita, near Fabriano, which came to the Brera in 1811. The artist's signature is legible and the distinct Tuscan character of his elegant painting with its soft colours is already evident.

Under the effect of the new developments in Tuscany, the Marches and Umbria gradually moved away from the Late Gothic style during the fifteenth century. This transition to the Renaissance is clearly seen in the panel painting depicting the *Virgin and Child with Angels*, attributed to the artist from Foligno, Bartolomeo di Tommaso (active 1425-1453), which came to the Brera from Pergola, in the Marches, in 1811. Although the overall composition is still Gothic, the influence of the spatial relationships that had been developed by Tuscan art may be noted in the more evident plasticity of the bodies.

The transition to the Renaissance had already been completed by Girolamo di Giovanni from Camerino, in the Marches (active 1449-1473), who trained in Padua in the milieu of Squarcione and the young Mantegna. He

66

painted the *Polyptych*, which came from Gualdo Tadino (in Umbria) in 1811, where the sharply-outlined volumes and the well-defined plasticity, even though of Paduan derivation, reveal that the influence of Piero della Francesca had now made itself felt.

The style of a possible pupil of Bartolomeo di Tommaso, Niccolò di Liberatore called Alunno, from Foligno (Umbria) (1430-1502) was less vigorous and more lyrically decorative. The gallery has a *Polyptych* by him, dated 1465, which came from Cagli in the Marches in 1811. This is an early work, clearly influenced by the Florentine Benozzo Gozzoli.

Hence in the vicinity of the Apennines between Umbria and the Marches there was a very active artistic movement in the Quattrocento. Its undisputed cornerstone was Piero della Francesca (already referred to above) (Sansepolcro, c. 1420-1492), whose very powerful influence went beyond the boundaries of the limited areas where he worked so as to resound not only all over Italy but also north of the Alps. The Brera is fortunate to possess one of Piero's most important works, the so-called *Brera Madonna* or *Madonna and Child with Federigo da Montefeltro*. Before painting this work Piero had worked in Ferrara and Rimini and on the famous cycle of frescoes in Arezzo. After basing his art on a rigorous concept of perspective and devising his own classical balance of form, light and colour, Piero frequented in Urbino, albeit intermittently, the court of Federigo da Montefeltro, where the protagonists of an extraordinary cultural movement gathered. The work was formerly placed on the high altar of the church of San Bernardino, just outside Urbino (it came to the Brera in 1811); it is not certain, however, if this was its original location. In the large well- preserved panel painting, the Virgin is seated on a throne in the nave of a church, while on her lap the Child is asleep; beside her are standing six saints and four angels. The donor, Federigo da Montefeltro, Duke of Urbino, kneeling on the right, is portrayed in profile; he is wearing armour, and only his helmet and gauntlets have been

Gentile da Fabriano, The Valle Romita Polyptych.

placed on the ground. In the shell of the apse is hanging an ostrich egg, a symbol of the Creation and the Virgin Birth and also, in a way, emblematic of the abstract geometrical concept of artistic form which was peculiar to Piero. The painting, in all likelihood, was executed between 1472 and 1474; the Duke's hands which are so realistic and thus in contrast with the rest of the work, have often been attributed to other artists working in Urbino, but who had a northern training, such as Pedro Berruguete or Joos van Gent. Due to the far-reaching implications of its spatial and architectural structure it is a fundamental, forward-looking work anticipating Bramante and Raphael, which is all the more remarkable for the care given to the decoration, the refinement of the details and the impassibility of the figures.

Shortly afterwards, perhaps around 1475, Luca Signorelli (Cortona, 1450-1523) painted a double-faced "standard," a panel that was intended for liturgical and processional use, for Santa Maria del Mercato in Fabriano. On one side is a delicate *Virgin and Child*, on the other a *Flagellation*. The latter takes place in a setting of classical architecture, with antique sculpture and reliefs; particular attention is paid to the anatomy of the bodies, which reflects the new Florentine and Pollaiolesque humanism grafted onto Piero della Francesca's innovations.

Further north is Ferrara, where in the Quattrocento there was one of the liveliest Italian schools, which was closely linked with what was going on in Padua. The leading artist was Cosma Tura (c. 1430-1495) who painted a small *Crucifix*, which has been cut out of a panel from an altarpiece depicting *Saint Jerome*. This work was originally in the Certosa in Ferrara; some panels from it are now in the National Gallery in London. The same sad

*Piero della Francesca, Madonna and Child
with Federigo da Montefeltro.*

fate, of separation and scattering, befell the *Griffoni Polyptych* by Francesco del Cossa (1436-1478), the second great Ferrarese artist. Executed in 1473 with the collaboration of the young Ercole de' Roberti, the polyptych was named after its patron, and was formerly in San Petronio in Bologna. After it had been broken up in the eighteenth century the frame was lost and the individual panels are now in various museums in different parts of the world, including the Vatican, Washington and London. In the Brera there are two small panels (purchased in 1894) representing *Saint Peter* and *Saint John the Baptist*. They are remarkable for the brilliance of the colours, the meticulousness of the details that depict the natural world and the vigorous modelling. The important influence that the *Griffoni Polyptych* had on a great deal of painting in Northern Italy is undeniable, both as a point of arrival of the Squarcionesque and Mantegnesque styles, but also as the starting point for new developments.

However, in the works now in the Brera it is not possible to sense the most characteristic aspect of Ferrarese art, in other words its passionate intensity. Also Ercole de' Roberti (c. 1451-1496), the third and youngest of the Ferrarese artists, who in the Palazzo Schifanoia frescoes and in the Griffoni predella is extremely harsh and violent, in the altarpiece in the Brera depicting the *Virgin and Child Enthroned with Saints*, from the church of Santa Maria in Porto in Ravenna, executed just before 1481, has taken a different approach. He creates calm, balanced luminosity in which the influence of Giovanni Bellini is perceptible. Under a four-sided loggia a throne decorated with antique bas-reliefs allows us to see, beyond slender columns, a pale blue landscape which might be Ravenna. The following generation, which now extended into the sixteenth century, was particularly active in Romagna, where it was centred on Ravenna and Forlì; it was influenced by both the Ferrarese artists and the up-and-coming Venetian school. The latter, and in particular Giovanni Bellini, had an important

69

Luca Signorelli, Flagellation.

Ercole de' Roberti, Virgin and Child Enthroned with Saints.

effect on an artist from Ravenna, Nicolò Rondinelli (c. 1450-c. 1510), who painted a number of works now in the gallery, including an altarpiece depicting the *Enthroned Virgin with Saints*, which came in 1811 from the church of San Domenico in Ravenna. From Bellini he derived a tender manner that has a modern flavour, yet is fluent without being mawkish. Marco Palmezzano, from Forlì (c. 1459-1539) was a more spirited painter, whose style derived to a large extent from Melozzo da Forlì and was also influenced by the Ferrarese school. This may be noted in the small but vigorous painting depicting the severed head of *Saint John the Baptist*, which came from a church at Cotignola, near Ravenna, in 1811.

Bologna, which in the second half of the Quattrocento was an offshoot of the Ferrarese school, in the latter part of that century and the early Cinquecento was strongly influenced by Umbrian artists, especially followers of Perugino. In the Brera there is a large *Annunciation* painted around 1505, from the church of San Francesco in Mantua in 1809, by Francesco Francia (c. 1450-1517), the Bolognese artist who had the greatest stylistic affinity with the Peruginesque school. The poetic tenderness, which at times becomes almost affected, is here expressed in the calm rhythm, in the intermittent gathering together—or, rather, moving apart—of the figures and in the important role that the vista of the landscape has in the painting.

The Ferrarese Lorenzo Costa (c. 1460-1535), active in Bologna at the same time as Francia and then in Mantua as Mantegna's successor in the position of court painter, was made of different stuff. The *Adoration of the Magi* in the gallery comes from the church of Santa Maria della Misericordia in Bologna, where it was the predella of an altarpiece which is still *in situ*; it depicts a variegated throng in procession, repeating a theme which is still typical of the Quattrocento.

The genius of Raphael (1483-1520), insofar as it can be explained, developed from the milieu of Perugia and Perugino. At first the son of Giovanni Santi was a loyal pupil of the Umbrian artist, in whose hands "the austere early classicism of Piero had become a style of détente, seeking easier naturalness and harmony in quiet, which too often verged upon inertia" (Freedberg, 1988). When in 1504 Raphael painted, complete with signature and date, the famous *Marriage of the Virgin*— one of the Brera's greatest treasures—he was, however, already developing his own individual style. The young "magister" (an independent painter)—as he was described for the first time in a document dated December 1500—after leaving Urbino towards the end of 1500 and moving to Perugia (or, according to some scholars, to Città di Castello), had learnt the art of painting large altarpieces from Perugino. Between 1501 and 1504 he painted at least three for Città di Castello. In fact, the *Marriage of the Virgin* is the last of these, and it was originally on an altar in the church of San Francesco. It was removed from there in 1798, and immediately presented to the Napoleonic general Giuseppe Lechi, who had "liberated" the town with his troops. It has been said, and this is a very likely explanation, that the townspeople offered the painting to the general in order to avert looting which they had reason to believe was imminent. Officially it was a gesture of gratitude. After changing hands a number of times the painting was finally purchased by the Viceroy Eugène de Beauharnais for the Brera in 1805.

The derivation of the picture from two works by Perugino, the fresco in the Sistine Chapel in the Vatican with the *Giving of the Keys to Saint Peter* (1481-82) and the altarpiece also depicting the *Marriage of the Virgin* in Caen Museum in France, formerly in Perugia Cathedral, has often been pointed out. In these paintings two groups of figures facing each other meet on the proscenium, behind which in all of them stands a temple in the form of a rotunda with pronaos, and in the background of all of them there is a vast landscape. Even the sentimental air of the figures in Raphael's work expresses the spirituality and ethereal grace of Umbrian art. Nevertheless, only Ra-

phael was capable of producing the classicism that was so much more natural than that of Perugino, avoiding his contrived languidness, and the almost romantic intensity which shines from the delicate faces of the personages. This would later be more fully expressed in large, vivid portraits. Note also the gilt frame, elegant and extremely elaborate; made in the Brera in 1857-58, it is an excellent example of nineteenth century Milanese ornamental work which sought to imitate the Renaissance style.

At the same time as Raphael's activity in Perugia, Timoteo Viti (1467-1525), who also came from Urbino, executed a painting depicting the *Virgin and Child with Saint Crescentino and Saint Vito* or *Saint Vitale*. Saint Crescentino is holding a banner with the coat of arms of Urbino. This painting, which is in a poor condition, came to the Brera from a church in Urbino in 1811; it has affinities with the *Casio Altarpiece* which the Lombard artist Boltraffio painted for a church in Bologna (it is now in the Louvre), and bears witness to Viti's training in that city in the orbit of Lorenzo Costa. Another painting by the artist, the *Virgin between Saint John the Baptist and Saint Sebastian*, which also came from Urbino in 1811, is evidence of his attempts to emulate Raphael and his serene classicism. The iconography is somewhat unusual: the Holy Child above is seen in the act of incarnation in the womb of the Virgin, who is receiving the Annunciation from the angel.

By the Roman school of Raphael, the influence of which rapidly spread to other regions of Italy after the artist's untimely death, the Brera possesses only five small paintings by one of its younger and more whimsical followers, the Florentine Perino del Vaga (born Pietro Buonaccorsi, c. 1501-1547). We are already in the so-called proto-Mannerist period, which is characterised by emotional and existential restlessness, sophisticated styles and contorted personalities. Possibly the predella of an altarpiece of 1534 which is now in Washington, or perhaps parts of a *Way of the Cross* which has now been lost, the small

Raphael, Marriage of the Virgin.

paintings by Perino (purchased in 1952) are charming examples of a mature Raphaelesque style that had almost been exhausted, and which was devoted to images devoid of moral or religious problems that merely constituted pleasant decoration.

Another more distant branch of the Raphaelesque style is that of Girolamo Genga, from Urbino (c. 1476-1551), known also for his activity as an architect. Executed in 1516, the large panel painting depicting the *Dispute over the Virgin Birth* comes from the church of Sant'Agostino in Cesena, where it was part of a large altar which was dismantled before the Napoleonic despoiling in 1809 and various parts of which are still *in situ*. Genga's Raphaelesque style is expressed more in the heritage of common values than in slavish imitation, to which his vigorous sense of plasticity could not adapt itself.

Meanwhile in Parma, in the same period, a very original artist was developing, who was able to amalgamate the artistic forms of his day with flexibility and intelligence. This painter was Antonio Allegri (c. 1489-1534) called Correggio, from the small town where he was born. The Brera possesses two of his early paintings, which were certainly executed before 1518, when he began his first large-scale commission, the *Camera di San Paolo* in Parma. The Mantegnesque inheritance of the youthful Correggio has often been stressed, but the small *Nativity* (purchased 1913), suffused with shadow, indicates a rapid transition to a "romantic" and idyllic sensibility which can only be described as Correggesque. Moreover, the most recent studies (Brown, 1981) see in this painting a specifically Leonardesque vein, which, it should be noted, was not merely academic but was vital and "enigmatic." The Leonardesque influence is even more evident in the other painting, the *Adoration of the Magi* (from the Archbishop's Palace in Milan, 1896), when the accentuated movement and the lighter palette are already harbingers of the great paintings in the Parmesan domes. Also in Emilia, in Ferrara, the large local

school did not die out but continued in the Cinquecento, without attaining the heights of the past, until the duchy came to an end in 1598. The Brera possesses a number of works by these sixteenth century Ferrarese artists. Just to mention a few names, it is worth referring to the large *Deposition* by Garofolo (Benvenuto Tisi, 1481-1559), a panel painting of 1527 from the church of Sant'Antonio in Ferrara, where in the figures evident Raphaelesque inspiration may be noted (Garofolo had actually met Raphael), as well as a picturesque landscape that is Venetian in style. The personality of Giovanni Luteri, called Dosso Dossi (c. 1480-1542), was more original. He was responsible for three paintings, *Saint John the Baptist*, *Saint Sebastian* and *Saint George* (these works came to the Brera in 1900 from a confraternity at Massalombarda in Romagna; the *Saint George* has also been attributed to the artist's brother, Battista). A romantic "at his own risk" as Jacob Burckhardt put it (1855), Dosso is often described as the Ferrarese alter ego of Titian, but the strong contrasts of light and shade that help to create such a dramatic atmosphere are entirely his own work.

We return briefly to Tuscany for a pair of "odd men out." The first is a tender *Saint Catherine of Alexandria* by the Florentine Giovanni Antonio Sogliani (1482-1544), who was active in the orbit of the old Lorenzo di Credi; the second is the *Portrait of Andrea Doria as Neptune* by Agnolo Bronzino (1503-1572). The latter painting has an interesting history. According to reliable sources it originally belonged to the Museo Giovio in Como, a collection of portraits of illustrious personages of the past and present which the Cinquecento humanist Paolo Giovio had assembled in his house and which still partially exists today in the Museo Civico in Como. This portrait was purchased in 1897. In 1540 (approximately the year in which it is believed the portrait was painted) Andrea Doria was the all-powerful lord of Genoa and had been proclaimed "father of the state"; quite clearly this mythological guise alludes to the sitter's

Girolamo Genga, Dispute over the Virgin Birth,
detail.

Antonio Allegri called il Correggio, Adoration of the Magi.

sea-faring prowess. The genre of the "iconic figure," in which a portrait of the head only is grafted onto an ideal, generic body, was very popular in ancient times: Bronzino revived it, after having obtained the idea from an unfinished statue by Baccio Bandinelli. However, he softened the figure with a chiaroscuro that was painterly in character, similar to that of Sebastiano del Piombo, thus avoiding his more typical style which was based on abstract stylisation devoid of sentimental expression.

With Bronzino we have reached the generation which is sometimes referred to as the high Maniera. Unfortunately, it is not possible for me to enlarge on this subject since the works that the Brera possesses by this generation and the following one, whether in Florence and Rome (Salviati, Zuccari, Sicciolante da Sermoneta), Bologna (Samacchini, Calvaert, Fontana) or Ferrara (Bastianino) were dispatched to many different places for storage in the nineteenth century, especially to churches in the Lombard provinces, after having fallen into disfavour with the critics. It can only be hoped that as soon as possible space for displaying the best of these paintings, which have now been rehabilitated by the art historians, will be found in the gallery. It is necessary, therefore, to proceed to an artist whose work marks the dissolution of the contrived exhibition of styles of the Mannerist period and the beginning of new aesthetic principles which were now sustained on a spiritual level by the Counter-Reformation in the second half of the Cinquecento.

Although Federico Barocci from Urbino (1535-1612) worked especially in Rome and central Italy, his notable links with Milan have recently been brought to light. One of

76

his greatest works is the altarpiece depicting the *Martyrdom of Saint Vitale*, which comes from the famous Basilica which bears the saint's name in Ravenna. It does, indeed, require something of an effort to imagine this lively, crowded painting in the Byzantine frame of San Vitale. On a rock at the bottom right it is signed and dated 1583; however we know that it had been started three years previously. Barocci was particularly slow and reflective in the execution of his works and he produced an enormous number of preparatory drawings. In 1761 Algarotti noted in his work—and what he wrote is still very fitting—"the tender sfumato with which the artist has been able to mix the colours, and the diaphanous air that he has given to the flesh." It is a fundamental painting for the Bolognese school which was to follow later on, that is to say the one of the Carraccesque reform.

This movement takes its name from the brothers Agostino (1557-1602) and Annibale Carracci (1560-1609) and their cousin Ludovico (1555-1619). Their reform, which took place in various cycles of frescoes and numerous altarpieces as well as in some precursors of genre painting, consisted in the search for a balance between idealisation of the form and naturalism, in other words between imitation of classical models and observation and study of the natural world. In the search for their own colouristic style the Carracci were strongly attracted by the Venetian artists, Correggio and Barocci, and above all they refused the cold cerebral Mannerism of their predecessors. Their ideals, which tended towards a total renaissance of art, were

perhaps most completely realised in the frescoes; nevertheless, among various works by them, the Brera possesses the equivalent, on a smaller scale, of a fresco cycle. These are three paintings, one by each artist, executed at the same time about 1593-94 for Palazzo Sampieri in Bologna (from where they were purchased in 1811), which at least permit the visitor to get an idea of their art. The paintings in question are the *Christ and the Samaritan Woman* by Annibale, *Christ and the Canaanite Woman* by Ludovico and *Christ and the Adulteress* by Agostino. The three subjects are linked in the sense that they refer to three different encounters between Christ and sinful women. The *Canaanite Woman* by Ludovico is particularly vigorous; in this work the rich, intense colour is moulded by accentuated sensibility in the meeting between the two protagonists. Also by Annibale is a *Self-portrait* from life, where the artist appears with his father and nephew Antonio. By Ludovico, the most solemn and austere of the three, there is a large gloomy *Saint Anthony Abbot Preaching* (it came from the church of Sant'Antonio in Bologna in 1809) and an *Adoration of the Magi* (from Crevalcore also in 1809).

After 1585 Annibale and Agostino went to Rome in order to work in the Galleria Farnese. This move took place shortly after that of a young Lombard, Michelangelo Merisi da Caravaggio (1573-1610). Annibale and Caravaggio, although they respected each other, were too far apart—even if they were not antithetical—in their artistic styles, to avoid giving rise to a conflict, which has long been part of the critical tradition. Since 1939 the

Guido Reni, Saint Peter and Saint Paul.

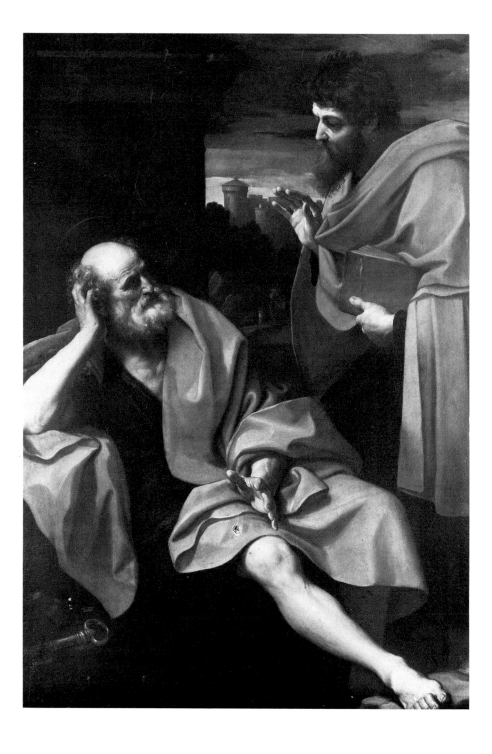

Guido Cagnacci, Death of Cleopatra.

Brera has possessed a masterpiece by Caravaggio, the *Supper at Emmaus*, which was formerly in the Casa Patrizi in Rome and was painted around 1606. The artist had already reached full maturity in the great cycle of paintings in San Luigi dei Francesi (1599-1602) and Santa Maria del Popolo (1601-02). In this painting, executed shortly before fleeing from Rome for the restless odyssey which took him to Naples, Malta and Sicily and finished so tragically at Port'Ercole, the artist embodied in a powerful manner one of the basic tenets of his beliefs, the revelation of God to man, in particular to the humble. In order to give physical shape to this perception of his the artist tried to achieve the greatest possible economy of means, which is clearly visible if we compare this work with another earlier *Supper at Emmaus* (c. 1596, National Gallery, London). All but abandoning colour he chose dark, burnt tones, gouging out with his unique light the faces of the protagonists; he reduced to a minimum the "still life" on the table, the beauty of which would be a possible source of distraction for the spectator; he obscured the surrounding room in the gloom of the background.

From Annibale Carracci and Caravaggio descend the two most important artistic movements of the first half of the Seicento, kept apart by their respective attitudes with regard to the great classics (Raphael first and foremost, then the ancients), but also, in a sense, linked by an analogous conflict concerning the humanisation of art. The Bolognese followers of the Carracci are well repre-

80 sented in the Brera; in any case they were to leave an indelible mark on two centuries of European classicism. A work which, according to recent studies, was executed in Rome around 1605 and sent from there to the Galleria Sampieri in Bologna (purchased 1811) is the painting depicting *Saint Peter and Saint Paul* by Guido Reni (1575-1640). It bears witness to the plasticity of chiaroscuro, a precise but transitory Caravaggesque period of Reni. The later and more famous work by Guido, his idealism and his classicism, is unfortunately not represented in this gallery. It was this aesthetic ideal and a taste for the classical landscape, from this moment onwards a driving force in European art, which inspired the once-famous and now unjustly forgotten *Dance of the Amoretti*, which also came from the Galleria Sampieri. Another good example of Bolognese classicism is *Abraham Driving Out Hagar and Ishmael* by Guercino (Giovanni Francesco Barbieri, 1591-1666), an artist who drew inspiration from Ludovico Carracci and the Venetian painters in his youth, creating masterpieces with a strong sense of colour and warm humanity, but who in his later years (to which this painting belongs; it was painted in 1657-58) took up a classical stance which showed Reni's influence and was characterised by a delicate, light palette. Another artist belonging to the Emilian Seicento (or rather to that in Romagna, since he was from Santarcangelo di Romagna, near Rimini), was Guido Cagnacci (1601-1681), who worked at the imperial court in Vienna. The *Death of Cleopatra* (donated in 1960) was one of his favourite themes; it was a fitting subject for a painter of subtle, delicate eroticism, endowed with a sense of rich, sensuous colour. This "Baroque" character is what most links Cagnacci to the artists of the Roman High Baroque. By Pietro da Cortona (Pietro Berrettini, 1596-1666), the most famous and significant of them, the gallery possesses an altarpiece which displays an extremely fresh sense of colour, depicting the *Virgin and Child with Saint John the Baptist, Saint Peter, Saint Catherine and Saint Felix of Can-

talice*. This signed work came from a church at Amandola in the Marches in 1811 and was painted around 1630-31.

In the other current in Roman art in the early 600, the Caravaggesque one, there was a large and motley array of painters, who were to varying degrees loyal followers of their master. The oldest of these is Orazio Gentileschi (1562-1638), by whom it is possible to admire a large altarpiece depicting *Saint Valerius, Saint Tiburtius and Saint Cecilia* (it came from the church of Santa Cecilia in Como in 1805). The light which emphatically models the figures and the dark background are the elements that are most typically Caravaggesque; otherwise the scene is composed with theatrical emphasis and is surmounted by an angel in flight.

Caravaggio had a more substantial following in Naples, where he stayed for a few months in 1606-07 and produced a few important works. The first Neapolitan to assimilate Caravaggio's innovations was Giovanni Battista Caracciolo called Battistello (c. 1570-1636). In fact, his *Christ and the Samaritan Woman*, with its characteristically dark background against which the figures only partially stand out with dramatic tension and where Christ's outstretched arm forms a solid plastic block with the figure of the Samaritan woman, was thought to be by Caravaggio himself when it came to the Brera in 1830. Another exponent of total naturalism was, during his long Neapolitan sojourn, the Spanish painter Jusepe de Ribera (1591-1652), by whom the Brera possesses a number of works, although their attribution to the artist is somewhat doubtful.

During the course of the century, even in Naples the Caravaggesque current began to lose momentum: an artist like Bernardo Cavallino (1616-1656), by whom there is a splendid *Immaculate Conception* (purchased 1956), certainly makes use of some naturalistic elements—the face, for example, which is far removed from orthodox formal idealisation—but generally speaking he is an adherent of a style which has become almost Baroque.

*Pietro da Cortona, Virgin and Child with Saint
John the Baptist, Saint Peter, Saint Catherine
and Saint Felix of Cantalice.*

Giovanni Battista Caracciolo called Battistello,
Christ and the Samaritan Woman.

Gaspare Traversi, Old Woman and the Urchin.

Also Mattia Preti called Cavaliere Calabrese (1613-1699) evolved, in the mature stage of his career, a manner that displayed the richly varied imagery of a great Baroque decorator. However a painting such as *Saint Peter and the Tribute Money* (gift of the Viceroy Eugène de Beauharnais, 1812) still contains very evident Caravaggesque features. These include not only the lighting, but also the composition, which brings to mind the *Calling of Saint Matthew* by Caravaggio in San Luigi dei Francesi and also the many variations on the tavern scene by Caravaggio's closest followers.

The same evolution may be observed in the art of Luca Giordano (1634-1705); the gallery has works from both his naturalist period and the Baroque one. From the first phase there is the *Portrait of a Chemist*, which is probably a self-portrait (it came to the Brera in 1855) forming part of a series of half-length figures of philosophers, which was inspired by a theme that Ribera had made fashionable. From the second phase there are two painted sketches for unidentified ceilings. Octagonal in shape and depicting *Joshua Halting the Sun* and the *Fall of the Walls of Jericho*, they may be dated after 1692. With their whirling impetuosity and passionate brushstrokes they are excellent representations of Giordano's personality, which already looks forward to the Settecento.

Also in Naples the style of Giovanni Lanfranco and Luca Giordano was inherited by Francesco Solimena (1657-1747), who painted great fresco cycles and altarpieces, which certainly allowed Neapolitan painting to finally make its mark on international Baroque. However, the Brera possesses two calm pictures by the artist, without whirling throngs: *Saint Leo the Great Meeting Attila* (note the unusual dulcification of the narrative, with the king of the Huns transformed into a sumptuously dressed and well-bred prince, whose train is held up by page) and *The Pope Presenting the Rule to Saint Benedict*. Both of these paintings came from the Bendictine monastery of San Giorgio Maggiore in Venice (they have been in the Brera since 1807) and it is possible to observe an evident affinity with contemporary Venetian art, which was also influenced by the heritage of Luca Giordano.

One last Neapolitan painter who was very much part of the Settecento remains to be considered: this was Giuseppe Traversi (1722?-1770). His activity in Naples was somewhat limited: in fact a large part of his output was produced in the Parma area. Moreover there is a great dichotomy of style and spirit between his religious works and the genre paintings which earned him greater fame. One of his genre paintings is the *Old Woman and the Urchin*, which is closely linked, perhaps excessively so, to a stereotyped image of the Neapolitan poor. Apart from this, the innovatory spirit of Traversi can be clearly perceived, with its combination of humour and desperation (this may be considered a peculiarly Neapolitan mixture) expressed in a style which is able to reflect at the same time a Caravaggesque heritage and enlightened modernity.

In Bologna a painter from the preceding generation, Giuseppe Maria Crespi called lo Spagnuolo (1665-1747) had developed a style in which the charm of realism and a painterly approach were combined with a remarkable sense of balance. A versatile artist, he applied his mordant and perceptive spirit to the most varied areas of painting, including scenes from day-to-day life, portraits, mythological themes and altarpieces. The Brera possesses examples of almost all these genres, but among these works a scene of day-to-day life is especially worth considering: the *Fair* (purchased 1916) which is closely related to a larger, more famous painting dated 1708, which is in the Uffizi. Note, together with the straightforward but sensitive observation of the chaotic market crowd, the fundamental elegance of this work; the figures are constructed with confidence and the areas of light are skilfully distributed. Crespi's sober, almost monochrome *Self-portrait* is a considerably more subdued affair.

Although the classical tradition in the Bolognese school soldiered on in the second half of Settecento, however, the brothers Ubaldo (1728-1781) and Gaetano (1734-1802) Gandolfi began to adopt a freer style with greater contrast of light and shade and vigorous brushstrokes, which was particularly influenced by the Venetian painters. In the fateful year of 1811 a painting by Ubaldo, dated 1768 on the reverse, depicting *Saint Francis Receiving the Stigmata* came to the Brera from a church at Cingoli in the Marches. The painting, which was recently returned to the gallery after being banished to the provinces for a long period, displays a glowing palette and a brilliant sense of decoration which are the essence of a sentimental tone brimming over with languor that has practically become romantic in character.

Meanwhile, Rome was experiencing a very different period involving a revival of classicism. An example of this is a brightly painted altarpiece by Pompeo Batoni (1708-1787) depicting the *Virgin and Child with Saint Joseph, Saint Zacharias, Saint Elisabeth and the Infant Saint John the Baptist* which was formerly in the Milanese church of Santi Cosma e Damiano alla Scala, now demolished. Painted about 1738-1740, it is clear evidence that, before the Neoclassical movement had really got under way, the painter was evolving in that direction. In fact, he was poised with masterly skill between the Roman Marattesque tradition and a new renaissance, of which he was in a sense the harbinger, of the classical world.

Other European Schools
Sandra Sicoli

The collection of paintings by artists from European countries apart from Italy owned by the Brera Gallery is fairly extensive, but many of these, either for reasons of space or because they have fallen into disfavour with the critics, have been sent to institutions outside the gallery or are in storage within the gallery itself: these works will not be dealt with in this publication. Generally speaking they are works whose quality varies somewhat, although they are all of interest and of disparate provenance. Hence the works on display have been very carefully selected, taking into account the origins and development of the gallery (as has been more thoroughly discussed in the introduction to this guide). The question of provenance is perhaps the most significant factor of this collection. In fact, unlike almost all the paintings in the Brera which came to Milan at the end of the eighteenth century and the mid-nineteenth century, following the dissolution of religious orders and the suppression of institutions including churches, convents and monasteries, the vast majority of the works by artists from other European countries came to the Brera at a later date during the course of the nineteenth and twentieth centuries, as a result of bequests, exchanges, purchases and gifts. Thus, in a sense, they contrast with the special character of the gallery, with its remarkable collection of religious paintings, which often have very large dimensions.

This is especially true of the Flemish and Dutch paintings of the end of the sixteenth and the early seventeenth centuries, many of which are quite small and are by minor artists or are ones that have not yet received adequate attention from scholars, or are by well-known artists whose particular merits are not sufficiently evident in these works to be worthy of mention. In general the subjects dealt with can be categorised as genre scenes, landscapes and seascapes and indeed it was no coincidence that in the postwar reorganisation of the gallery these paintings were hung together in two small rooms, thereby stressing the unique character of this collection. It was decided to exhibit them in chronological order, although the works of a number of artists who were active at the end of the eighteenth and the beginning of the nineteenth centuries, such as Knoller, Mengs, Reynolds, Lawrence and Proud'hon, are displayed in the section pertaining to the nineteenth century since they are more closely related to the artistic vicissitudes of that century.

It is, therefore, my intention to begin with the panel painting depicting the *Adoration of the Magi* by the Master of the Virgo inter Virgines, thus named by the German art historian Friedländer who in 1906 reconstructed this artist's *oeuvre* by referring to about ten works, beginning with the painting of the Virgin surrounded by the virgin saints (*Virgo inter Virgines*) in the Rijksmuseum, Amsterdam. Still today little is known about this artist, who is known to have been active from 1480 to 1495 and whose career commenced in the town of Delft. Also active as an engraver, he certainly had a flourishing workshop and numerous followers and he was an important link between the local schools which existed in the southern part of the Netherlands. The Brera painting, which used to be catalogued in the gallery guides as *Dutch School of the Sixteenth Century*, is one of his first works, in which formal motifs borrowed from the Master of Flémalle and Rogier van der Weyden are evident, for example the angels with swirling robes who hold up the curtain behind the Virgin and the use of features that are clearly architectural in character, such as the arch that forms the proscenium. The composition is rigidly symmetrical and the figures are divided into two separate groups; this structure was then repeated in later works. Typical of the Flemish iconographical tradition is the presence in the foreground of the greyhound, as well as the great attention which is given to the meticulous depiction of fabrics, in this case the brocaded satin of the Magi king.

By a Flemish artist, Jan de Beer, born in

Jan de Beer, Adoration of the Magi.

Peter Paul Rubens, Last Supper.

Antwerp, or at least he was a Master of the Artist's Guild in that city, is the triptych of the *Nativity*, the *Adoration of the Magi* and the *Rest on the Flight to Egypt*. This panel painting can certainly be considered to be his masterpiece, even though some scholars believe that it is not entirely by the artist's hand. Probably executed between 1515 and 1517 for the church of Santa Maria dei Servi in Venice, the painting, which was believed to be by Dürer, was sent to the Brera in 1808 where it was displayed with an attribution to Civetta (Herri met de Bles), one of the many Italianised Netherlandish painters, and then with the label "Master òf Antwerp of 1520." The sumptuousness of the decorative motifs, the search for colouristic effects and the presence of excessively elaborate Late Gothic and Renaissance architecture would seem to indicate that this was an important commission. Together with other contemporary artists, such as Van Orley or Gossaert, de Beer displayed a taste for antiquity which he had inherited from sketch-books by North European artists or from North Italian prints, but at the same time he made use of iconographic models which occurred very frequently in the Flemish tradition, for example the old king kneeling before the Virgin; and he created new ones, such as the shepherds dancing round a fire, an invention which was then used both by North European artists and Italian ones, such as Savoldo.

It is also worth noting the interesting tempera painting which depicts *Saint Luke Painting the Virgin*, by an anonymous painter from Antwerp of the sixteenth century, from the collection which Cardinal Cesare Monti left to the Archbishop's Palace in 1650 and which in part came to the Brera in 1811. This is the only replica of a lost painting which was executed by the well-known Netherlandish artist Quentin Metsys for the confraternity of Saint Luke in Antwerp; it depicts a rare episode in the iconography of the saint.

From a later period, but still with Northern European provenance, is a group of five paintings by Rubens, Van Dyck, Rembrandt

Dirk van Santvoort, Portrait of a Young Man.

and Jordaens which the Brera received from the Louvre in exchange for five works by Italian artists (the gallery sent to Paris the *Casio Altarpiece* by Boltraffio, *Saint Stephen Preaching* by Carpaccio, *Saint Bernardino da Siena and Saint Louis of Toulouse* and *Saint Bonaventura and Saint Anthony of Padua*, two panels that were part of a polyptych from Gardone Val Trompia by Moretto and the *Holy Family* by Marco d'Oggiono). The *Last Supper* by Peter Paul Rubens was executed in 1631 and 1632 after it had been commissioned by Catherine Lescujer for the altar of the Holy Sacrament of the church of Saint Romuald in Malines, in order to commemorate her father. It is not entirely by the artist's hand, as is, in fact, the case with many paintings by Rubens, who was obliged to leave much of the execution of his works to his assistants in order to cope with the huge demand for them which had been stimulated by his fame.

The *Last Supper* was painted shortly after the artist had stayed at the court of Philip IV in Madrid, where he had had the opportunity to study the works of Titian in the Escorial. But apart from that of the Venetian artist, there is the evident influence of other Italian artists, for example Veronese and Caravaggio, whose work Rubens had observed attentively during his Italian journeys. Together with this painting there were also two predellas depicting the *Entry of Christ into Jerusalem* and *Christ Washing the Disciples' Feet*, which, however, were sent to the Museé des Beaux-Arts in Dijon, where they are still to be found.

By another Flemish painter, Van Dyck, who was Rubens's favourite pupil, the Brera possesses a painting with a religious theme, the *Virgin and Child and Saint Anthony*, probably executed between 1627 and 1632 and the *Portrait of a Noblewoman*, formerly known as the *Portrait of Amalia von Solms*, princess of Orange and wife of the governor of the Netherlands. Since it does not bear any resemblance to the official portraits of the princess, it can only be assumed that it is the portrait of a Flemish lady connected with the court in Brussels; it can be dated to 1634 or 1635. The artist, who was born in Antwerp, from 1621 stayed for about six years in Italy, where he was influenced in a decisive manner by the art of this country. After being appointed court painter for the king of England, Charles I, he excelled above all as a portraitist; in this field his technical ability reached its greatest heights, producing not only a psychological analysis of the sitters, but also the official image that was required for public consumption.

By the Dutch painter and engraver Rembrandt there is a *Portrait of a Young Woman*, which can be dated to around 1632 and probably depicts the artist's youngest sister, Lijsbeth, who also appears in other paintings. Rembrandt, who had settled in Amsterdam only a year previously after leaving his native Leiden for good, thanks to his great skill as a portraitist managed to make a name for himself among the bourgeoisie of the city, thus becoming a fashionable artist. It has been estimated that between 1631 and 1633 he painted more than fifty portraits. Rembrandt's constant concern, besides the renewal of his iconography, which is frequently difficult to interpret, was the fascinatingly incisive representation of the sitter's state of mind, which created a genre of painting with a lavish use of chiaroscuro that shows the influence of North European representatives of the Caravaggesque style, such as Van Honthorst.

Of the group of paintings that came from the Louvre, the *Sacrifice of Isaac* by the Flemish painter Jordaens is also worthy of note. Born in Antwerp and student of Adam Van Noort, he favoured a style of painting with lurid colours and strong contrasts of light and shade. A contemporary of Rubens (with whom he worked a number of times) and Van Dyck, he painted religious and mythological themes — preferring those with profane subjects, such as banquets and concerts — with a more expressive style which had fewer intellectual overtones and was decidedly more realistic than that of the other two artists.

By the Dutch artist Van Santvoort, a refined portraitist who was influenced by Rembrandt, there is an important painting, signed and dated 1643, *Portrait of a Young Man*, purchased by the gallery in 1927. Finally I would like to refer to two paintings by the French artist Pierre Subleyras that are particularly interesting from a historical point of view. Together with a work by Bottani and one by Batoni, they formed the first group of paintings in the Brera Gallery. They are the *Vision of Saint Jerome* (1739) and *Christ on the Cross between Saint Eusebius, Saint Philip Neri and Mary Magdalene* (1744), executed for the Milanese church of Santi Cosma e Damiano, suppressed in 1796 and replaced by the Teatro Filodrammatici. These two paintings were commissioned from Subleyras when he had become a very famous artist; in fact he was elected to the Accademia di San Luca in Rome in 1740. The paintings in the Brera are a significant example of his great skill as a painter of imposing, monumental altarpieces, which are deliberately idealised, anti-expressive and anti-realistic.

The Nineteenth and
Twentieth Centuries
Luisa Arrigoni

The nineteenth century paintings that have been on display in the Brera Gallery for the last forty years are only a very poor reflection of the size and character of the collection of works of art from the last century which the gallery owns. At least until the 1920s, with the exclusion of numerous paintings and sculptures lent in 1903 to the City of Milan for the new Modern Art Gallery, they were hung in double rows on the walls of the last large rooms of the gallery, or even placed on easels. A prestigious beginning that was certainly at a European level was the marble monument, with its delicate, velvety *Graces*, executed in 1826 by Bertel Thorvaldsen in memory of Andrea Appiani; now deprived of its dignity it is, unfortunately, half-hidden in the entrance-hall of the gallery.

During the course of the nineteenth century the Academy of Fine Arts of Milan—to which the gallery was officially linked as an institution until 1882—with its school and its popular annual exhibitions where the works of pupils and teachers, both from Milan and other academies, were displayed, as well as those of full-time painters, professional sculptors and amateurs, played a fundamental role in the history and ideological and social development of the art of the day. In this context the modern collections were formed and expanded almost until the end of the century. They were added to year by year by the works that had won various prizes (Grand Prize, State Prizes, Roman Pensioners, Canonica Prizes, Mylius, Prince Umberto and so on), works donated by the artists themselves or by the few collectors who were interested in contemporary art (for example Count Stefano Stampa, step-son of the writer Alessandro Manzoni) and works purchased by the Ministry of Education with the so-called Exhibition Fund. The result was a rich collection that was of almost unmanageable dimensions, which, nevertheless, was confusing and incomplete if its scope was that of giving a general outline of painting in Italy in the nineteenth century.

These limits of the collection were due to its academic origins and the fact that it was almost entirely Lombard in composition. This was worsened by the situation of great confusion which was created when the gallery was separated from the Academy and all the works of art of the past, together with the nineteenth century works, went to the former institution, which, however, continued to display those works which were still the property of the Academy. Although these were handed back in the course of time in an improvised manner, since there was no overall planning, problems connected with the exhibition of these works have remained due to shortage of space and the restricted range of works available. The succession of directors in the nineteenth century, stimulated by the desire to turn the Brera Gallery into an institution having national status in which the development of Italian painting from the fifteenth century to the beginning of the twentieth century was to be the main theme, avoided the thorny problem of the nineteenth century collection by continually reducing the number of works on display. In 1908, besides the one hundred and eighteen paintings donated by Stefano Stampa, there were more than a hundred students' works and examination pieces from the Academy; but by 1924 the works exhibited had been reduced to little more than a hundred; in the 1938 reorganisation they were further cut down to around sixty and the discarded works, which were transformed into what might be termed "furnishings of honour," were banished to such dreary places as the offices of the Procurator and the Law Officers in the Courts, the Revenue Office, the Police Headquarters, the Prefecture and the Milan Army Headquarters, as well as the Chamber of Deputies and the Senate building in Rome. The quality of the works on show was varied in accordance with the tastes of the day, while attempts were made to fill the gaps (the moment came when it was felt to be reprehensible that there were no Macchiaioli) with purchases and gifts to this end. Thus when the gallery was reopened after the Second

Andrea Appiani, Apollo and Daphne.

World War, only a brief, carefully selected anthology of forty-two works was on display, which succinctly outlined the history of art in the nineteenth century from Neoclassicism to Romanticism, Realism/Verism.

Today the situation is more complex: a number of works which were on loan have been returned, there has been a fresh appraisal of the well-stocked storerooms in the gallery and the sculptures and plaques, all nineteenth century, which crowd the stairways, courtyard, loggia and corridors of the building have been restored, while an increasing number of exhibitions dedicated to Italian nineteenth century art have given prominence to alternative artists and historical perspectives. Thus, despite the lack of space which makes periodic rotation of the works necessary, it has been possible for visitors to acquire a deeper knowledge of the nineteenth century collection. It is sincerely hoped that when the rebuilding of Palazzo Citterio has been completed it will be possible to exhibit it in a more methodical manner.

For the time being the nineteenth century in the Brera begins with a number of works by Andrea Appiani (Milan 1753-1817); the most famous exponent of the Neoclassical movement in Milan, he had been trained in the milieu, which was Austrian in its severity, of the architect Giuseppe Piermarini, who among his numerous commissions had rebuilt the austere college of the Jesuits in the Palazzo di Brera, converting it into the Academy of Fine Arts. When the French arrived in Milan he became an artist of European stature; after 1805 he obtained the prestigious title of *premier peintre* (Court Painter) of the new kingdom, the honours and commissions came flooding in and he became, among other things, Commissioner for Fine Arts and promoter and arbiter, together with Giuseppe Bossi, secretary of the Academy, of the plan for the requisitioning of the works of art from various departments which were to form the basis of the new art gallery. *Apollo and Daphne, Apollo and Hyacinthus* and *Apollo's Chariot* were executed in 1778-1800. Together with *Apollo and Clizia* and *Apollo and Marsyas* (these two works have been on loan to the Civica Galleria d'Arte Moderna since 1903, which is an example of the Solomonic rigour with which the nineteenth century collection of art works was split up), they formed part of the fresco cycle with delicate and atypical Neoclassical features depicting the *Stories of Apollo* which Appiani painted in the house of Count Giacomo Sannazzari della Ripa, a very wealthy man who at the turn of the century built up an exceptional, albeit somewhat heterogeneous, art collection. The building then became the property of Giuseppe Prina and was plundered during the tragic riots of 1814 which led to the lynching of the hated Minister of Finance; the frescoes, which were partly damaged, were detached, transferred to canvas and taken to the Brera.

Totally different due to its courtly, imperial tone with an unashamedly ideological content is the lunette, with the splendid original frame, depicting the *Olympus* or *the Coronation of Jupiter*, where the myth is transformed, with an ample dose of flattery, into a noble parade celebrating—by means of a facile allegory that displays superficiality—the greatness of the emperor. The cultural interests of Appiani, who was not only passionately fond of music but was also a skilled musician himself, are demonstrated by the splendid portrait, shadowy and romantic before its time, of *Ugo Foscolo* dated 1801-02 (it was purchased thanks to Giuseppe Bertini, who became the first director of the gallery in 1882) in which there are vague stylistic affinities with English painting, while the oval *Self-portrait* is a small masterpiece that is spontaneous almost to the point of carelessness, with the poignancy and sparkle of a passage from Mozart.

This work should be compared with a number of *Self-portraits* by the early artists active in the milieu of the Brera Academy in the late eighteenth and early nineteenth centuries in order to fully savour the atmosphere of the period: there is the one which still has a wholly Settecento charm, à la Chardin, painted by Giuliano Traballesi (Florence 1727-Milan 1812), donated by the artist in 1805, but apparently executed about twenty years previously, the one in the manner of Mengs by Martin Knoller (Steinbach 1725-Milan 1804) and the austere, almost Jacobinic one by Domenico Aspari (Milan 1745-1831) right up to the agitated, febrile *Self-portrait* by Giuseppe Bossi (Busto Arsizio, near Varese 1777-1815), who was the memorable secretary of the Academy and friend of Canova, whom he had met in Rome in 1795 together with Angelica Kauffmann and the eccentric Felice Giani. Not only a painter, but also a man of the world, collector and fascinating orator, he was deeply involved in the promulgation of Neoclassical art, of which he was both critic and historian. The *Self-portrait* in the Brera, one of the many which the artist painted, dates to 1814, when the illness which was soon to be the cause of his death had already left evident traces of consumption, which are, however, overridden by the introspective intensity of his gaze, while the unusual composition and handling of the paint are startlingly modern.

The nearby *Portrait of Andrea Canova* should on no account be missed; he was one of the first exponents—and perhaps the most important one—of the new Neoclassical style, not only in Italy, but also in the whole of Europe, extolled by his contemporaries, for whom "he was little less than a divinity, the supreme expression of the style" (M. Praz). With his personal prestige he obtained, after 1815, the restitution to Italy of many of the works of art which had been purloined by Napoleon. The portrait, which was painted by Sir Thomas Lawrence (Bristol 1769-London 1830), may be admired for its fluid brushwork, light palette and delightfully bold, spontaneous manner which owes a great deal to the influence of Reynolds.

The collection of Neoclassical art in the Brera could not lack the imposing *Portrait of Giambattista Sommariva* by Pierre Paul Prud'hon (Cluny 1758-Paris 1823) donated in 1873 by Countess Emilia Sommariva, which is anglicized in the wholly unaffected natural pose and the landscape setting with allusions to events in the sitter's life. Sommariva, who from 1800 to 1802 was the real lord of Milan and managed to build up an immense fortune which made him one of the richest men in Europe, is sitting in the garden of his villa at Tremezzo on Lake Como (now the Villa Carlotta) where he had collected works by his beloved Canova, Thorvaldsen and Appiani and also by Hayez and Migliara, together with paintings from the past. Behind him there are two very famous sculptures by Canova, *Palamede* (1803-04) and *Terpsichore* (1811).

The display in this section of a number of landscapes by Marco Gozzi (San Giovanni Bianco, near Bergamo 1759-Milan 1839) is chronologically correct. At any rate, because of his date of birth and his presence in Milan—the largest centre of Neoclassical art after Rome—he is comparable with the artists that have just been mentioned, even though his concentration on landscapes, which was alien to the Neoclassical credo and certainly not typical of this movement, isolated him and caused him to carry on the artistic traditions of the Settecento oblivious to new developments. Rightly considered by the nineteenth century critics to be "the Nestor of the Lombard landscapists," he invariably took part in the exhibitions at the Brera from 1813 to 1835 and his views, which are always true-to-life, emanating serenity and "good taste" together with order and stability mixed with down-to-earth enlightenment, were only slightly updated in his later years with some imperceptible Romantic elements. Regarding landscape painting, whether as perspective views, landscapes from life or imaginary ones and historical landscapes (which were produced in great abundance during the nineteenth century), it is only possible to regret the absence of works by Migliara, Giuseppe Bisi, Federico Moja and D'Azeglio which are in the Brera's possession, but which have been out on loan for years to adorn various public offices.

Francesco Hayez, Bathsheba Bathing.

There is a very extensive collection of paintings by Francesco Hayez (Venice 1791-Milan 1862). This artist brings us to historical Romanticism, which was propagated in Europe after the fall of Napoleon and the collapse of the myth of the universal hero who was both the protagonist and creator of history. Due to political, social and cultural factors, in Italy this coincided with, in the words of C. Maltese, the "patriotic and sentimental" painting of the Risorgimento, the movement for the political unification of the country.

Hayez was "leader of the school of History Painting, which the National thought demanded in Italy: the artist who had most developed... a sense of the ideal" and a "democratic genius" as he was described somewhat arbitrarily by the Italian nationalist Giuseppe Mazzini. He was the favourite portraitist of the nobility and upper middle-classes in Milan, including both the liberals who were committed to the struggles of the Risorgimento and the conservatives who were pragmatically loyal to Austria, right from the time of his first Milanese triumph with the famous *Pietro Rossi* of 1820 — although his first commissions under the aegis of patrons such as Count Leopoldo Cicognara and Antonio Canova were in Venice and Rome. He worked successfully for many years, continuing to exert, as professor of painting at the Brera, a strong influence on Italian art.

The *Group Portrait of the Borri Stampa Family*, bequeathed by Stefano Stampa to the Academy in 1879, was painted during Hayez's first sojourn in Milan (1822-23). It centres on the figure of Manzoni's second wife, who had recently been widowed, and who was portrayed with her small son, brother and mother; the group — united by composed but solid bonds of affection that were evident in the self-effacing manner in which they had gathered together — did not meet with the approval of the client, who required a number of modifications, which are still visible if the work is observed with raking light. Thus an urn, to which no one was paying any attention, was removed from the column, the over-dark landscape and the woman's face were altered. Twenty years later there were the same splendid toned-down colours and the same outstanding civility of manners and sentiment in the portraits — which have too frequently been reproduced for them to have been painted as works for private consumption without an official role — of *Alessandro Manzoni* (1841) and *Teresa Borri Stampa* (1847-49, although the official date was 1848). Equally popular was the *Self-portrait at the Age of Fifty-seven*, the most famous of the many self-portraits which the artist painted, portentously signed and dated "Fran.co Hayez — Italian from the city of Venice — painted this work: 1848"; this was the crucial year of the Risorgimento. On the other hand, the *Kiss. Youthful Episode. Fourteenth Century Costumes* — this is the complete title — was painted in 1859, which was a momentous year for the unification of Italy, in an atmosphere of intense patriotic fervour.

Perhaps the most reproduced work of Italian nineteenth century art, it is certainly the most popular, endowed with a visual charm that is so strong that it had an echo in Luchino Visconti's film *Senso*. This medium-sized painting, with brilliant enamel colours and unhackneyed theatrical poses, was immediately interpreted as a good omen for the growth of the new nation: "from this affectionate kiss comes forth a sturdy, sincere generation which takes life as it comes and makes it fruitful with love of beauty and truth" (F. Dall'Ongaro).

The various stages of Hayez's astonishing career are illustrated by a number of important works. For example, there is the *Portrait of Carlo della Bianca* of 1822 with its unusual sense of intimacy. *Bathsheba Bathing* of 1834 was an academic exercise that had affinities with the purist movement of that period and Bolognese classicism of the Seicento. It allowed the artist to deal under a biblical guise with the theme of the female nude, which was obviously a success from a commercial point of view. *Melancholy* of 1859, which is displayed next to the *Kiss*, is equally allusive

Gerolamo Induno, Sad Foreboding.

with the silky figure of the woman in a light blue satin dress. The *Vase of Flowers on the Window-sill of a Harem* of 1881, a lush still-life of flowers in an exotic environment, represents a real victory against all the odds for the ninety-year-old painter.

Involuntarily antithetical to Hayez's art was the painting of Giovanni Carnovali called Piccio (Montegrino, near Varese 1804-Cremona 1873), the most genuinely Romantic Italian painter: his intense sentiments, the complexity of light and shade and the splendid impasto which had the density of Constable's painting were taken up by such *Scapigliatura* (a Lombard literary and artistic movement of the late nineteenth century) painters as Tranquillo Cremona, Daniele Ranzoni and the sculptor Giuseppe Grandi. His *Portrait of* *Signora Ghisoli*, donated in 1931 by the Associazione Amici di Brera was painted, according to the passionate comment by O. Maltese which, despite being somewhat overemphatic, is quite fitting, "with the same calm confidence that Titian had, but he was a Titian who had descended from the heights of his imperial throne and had mingled, obtaining a tinge of melancholy from it, with the bourgeoisie or provincial aristocracy of Lombardy and Veneto in the early nineteenth century." Giuseppe Molteni (Affori, near Milan 1800-Milan 1867), who restored such famous paintings as the *Marriage of the Virgin* by Raphael and the *Dead Christ* by Mantegna, was an art consultant and dealer, besides being the painter of famous and much sought after portraits in very detailed historical settings and scenes

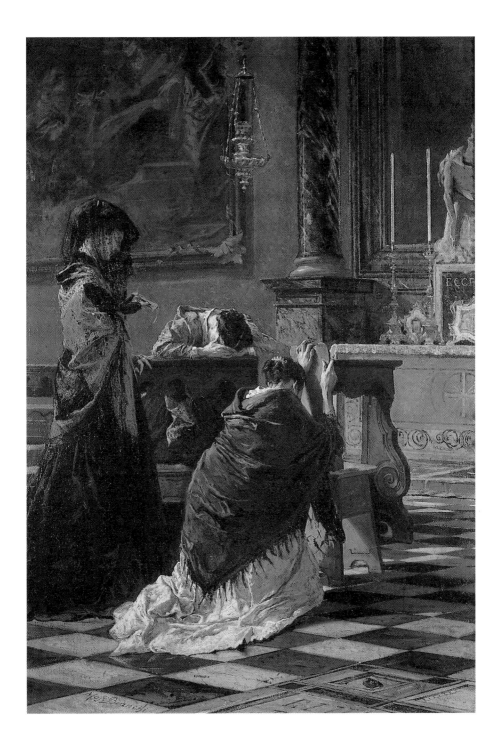

Mosè Bianchi, The Brothers are on the Field.

of contemporary life "inspired by the distressing or pathetic vicissitudes which afflict human beings" (A. Caimi). With Molteni we have returned once again to a fashionable, commercially successful artist whose patrons were upper-class and socially ambitious. In his *Death of a Child*, signed and dated 1845, donated to the Brera in 1927, there is a miserable little room sharply painted with every possible detail carefully depicted; it is a perfect example of that edifying and emotional genre of painting that had much in common with the popular serialized fiction published in the newspapers of the day.

On a considerably higher plane, and destined to have a much more far-reaching effect, was the painting of the brothers Domenico (Milan 1815-1878) and Gerolamo Induno (Milan 1825-1890). Domenico, pupil at the Brera of Luigi Sabatelli and then Hayez, started with excessively ornate history painting, evolving to genre painting with works in which the authenticity of settings and sentiment was sustained and motivated by overt patriotic aspirations which were legitimized when he participated in the Cinque Giornate (a rebellion against the Austrians in 1848) in Milan and his subsequent exile in Switzerland and Tuscany. Gerolamo was educated with his brother and was even more involved in the struggle for national independence: in 1849 at Villa Barberini in Rome he received as many as twenty-two wounds and he also took part in Garibaldi's campaign. He was one of the first examples of what we might describe today as a war artist; thus Hayez's nobly patriotic history painting was transformed into an art which recorded current events and trends and in which there was ample space for family sentiments, attention to the precision of the minor points and curiosity regarding details of day-to-day life. In *Sad Foreboding*, also known by the more explicit title of the *Fiancée of a Soldier in Garibaldi's Army*, painted in 1862 for the Brera exhibition and on that occasion purchased by the Minister of Education, the patriotic theme and the commitment to the ideals of the Risorgimento are indirect-

ly revealed by what at first sight might appear to be insignificant allusions: the reproduction of Hayez's *Kiss*, the photograph of the barricades and the bust of Garibaldi. Thus patriotism and personal sentiments are combined in a delicate and convincing Realist painting.

The artistic origins of Federico Zandomeneghi (Venice 1841-Paris 1917), who was a friend of Diego Martelli and the Macchiaioli, were linked to the Realist movement. In the *Poor on* the *Steps of the Monastery of the Ara Coeli* he showed himself to be socially committed, while later in Paris, where he spent the rest of his career as a successful, if minor, Impressionist, he adopted a lighter palette and light-hearted themes, with the total dedication to female beauty which he shared with Renoir.

Another Venetian was Giacomo Favretto (Venice 1849-1887). His painting, which was very successful commercially after a beginning which was rigorously Realist—as was the case with various Macchiaioli artists—in the end was reduced to little more than the virtuosity of the brushwork and lively anecdotes. These works were limited in scope, for example in *The Mouse* of 1878, which made him very popular, and *Vandalism* (*Poor Ancients!*) of 1880, which earned him the Principe Umberto prize.

Not very different was the career and style of the exuberant Mosè Bianchi (Monza, near Milan 1840-1904), who, like Favretto, painted Neo-Settecento scenes in the manner of Fortuny and Meissonier which also met with commercial success in France, thanks to the dealer Goupil, and also genre painting, portraits, townscapes, seascapes and views of lakes in a vast output which is bewildering in its variety. Some of his works displayed real artistic merit, such as the simple, severe *The Reader* of 1867, painted when he was in the second year of the Oggioni boarding-school. This was a foretaste of the more elaborate and famous *The Brothers are on the Field*. *Memory of Venice* of 1869, a belated patriotic work associated with the third war of inde-

Giovanni Fattori, Red Wagon.

pendence and the liberation of Venice that shows the artist in the best light, confirming his excellent capacity for handling colour and tone. However, other works belonging to what can only be described as the choirboy-sacristy school are today quite intolerable, such as the *Eve of a Religious Feast* of 1864 and the *Blessing of the House* of 1870, which were both recently returned from the Revenue Office in Milan where they had been on loan.

A totally different matter was the brief career of Federico Faruffini (Sesto San Giovanni, near Milan 1833-Perugia 1869), a restless figure who never fully realised himself. Although his family compelled him to study law at the university of Pavia, he preferred to attend the courses held by the painter Trécourt at the municipal art school in that city, as well as those of Giuseppe Bertini in Milan. In him are summed up in a contradictory manner— as is evident in his ambitious, though not wholly successful, picture *The Poet's Love. Sordello and Cunizza* of 1864—the historical Romanticism of the recent past, the style of Realism and experiments with light effects and colour, which would be taken up again shortly afterwards by the artists of the *Scapigliatura* movement. With Tranquillo Cre-

mona and Daniele Ranzoni, who frequented writers, poets and musicians such as Rovani, Praga, Catalani and Boito, the study from life became the opportunity for experiments and was identified with the most extreme research into light effects, carried out with a decadent spirit and taste, which aimed at dissolving the very outlines and forms in a style which was wholly based on atmosphere, with thick, rapidly applied paint, dominated by an overwhelming emotional content. In *Maternal Love*, on loan from the City of Milan collections, and the Portrait of *Teresa Sonzogno on her Deathbed* by Tranquillo Cremona, real images and ghostly evanescent creatures find a wholly superficial balance with effects that are somewhat repulsive, while the twilit, delicately melancholy *Portrait of Signora Biraghi Pavesi* by Daniele Ranzoni (Intra, on Lake Maggiore 1843-1889) may be appreciated for the fluid handling of the paint and the quiet sense of intimacy.

On quite another plane with regard to the eclectic and contradictory Realism of the Lombard and Venetian painters was the unitary, genuinely Realist experience of the Macchiaioli group, which in Florence between 1850 and 1860, in revolt against the history painting and purism of the academy, as-

Silvestro Lega, The Pergola.

serted itself by radically renewing the painting of the day. Besides the Tuscans Serafino de Tivoli, Cristiano Banti, Raffaello Sernesi, Telemaco Signorini, Giovanni Fattori and Odoardo Borrani, the movement included the Roman Giovanni Costa, Vito d'Ancona from the Marches, the Neapolitan Giovanni Abbati and the Veronese Vincenzo Cabianca. In it the democratic ferment that had accompanied the liberal movement for unification produced a new aesthetic consciousness, which was based on an overriding interest in the real world, landscape and contemporary life with the exclusion of any literary or historical references. Moreover, feelings of sincerity and spontaneity of expression were conveyed by patches or blobs of pure colour (*macchie*) instead of chiaroscuro, by the execution of paintings from life—in *plein air* and if possible in direct sunlight in order to observe the effects of strong contrasts of light and shade—preferring the distant viewpoint from which details could be disregarded, and by the use of strong, bright colours.

The most outstanding figure of the group for his artistic and ethical commitment was Giovanni Fattori (Leghorn 1825-Florence 1908) who still today is recognised as being the leading Italian Realist painter. Endowed with an uncommon simplicity of sentiment, Fattori chose to limit himself to depicting ordinary people and country life, which he alternated with episodes of war and figures of soldiers. But for him the epic of the Risorgimento was not something to be celebrated with fanfares and heroic gestures, rather it was an onerous duty, a tough everyday task. He painted life behind the lines, the wagons with the wounded and the supplies, while his battles involved the sweat and suffering of men and animals, fatigue, time spent waiting for orders and solitary patrols. With the same commitment and compassion and with a terse, succinct style which consisted of strong colours and brusque, discontinuous brushwork, he painted landscapes of the Maremma (a marshy coastal area in southern Tuscany) and the sea and countryside around Leghorn, peasants, stone-breakers, women carrying water, oxen, horses, carts and forlorn grounded boats. Thus in the painting of *Prince Amadeo Wounded at Custoza* of 1870 the artist depicts only a break in the bloody and inauspicious battle after the ambulance has arrived. In the *Red Wagon* of 1887, one of his most successful paintings of the Maremma, the weary, archaic calm of the white oxen and the herdsman with his face scorched by the unbearable midday heat is made tangible by the strong contrasts of light and shade and by the monumental simplicity of the scene.

Silvestro Lega (Modigliana, in Romagna 1826-Florence 1895), only joined the Macchiaioli after a strict academic training in Romantic and Purist circles. In fact, it was this experience which allowed him to distinguish himself for the lucidity of his vision and a serene, balanced choice of colour. *The Pergola* of 1868, also known as *Early Afternoon*, donated by the Amici di Brera in 1931, is an exquisitely painted work which captures the spectator's attention with the almost mythical tranquillity of its small, closed world and with the dazzling light which can be compared to that of Monet's early work.

Clarity of vision and intensity of involvement similar to that of Fattori and Lega, but with totally different undertones, are to be found in the *Spring Pastures* by Giovanni Segantini (Arco, near Trento 1858-Engadine, Switzerland 1899), a painter who was Divisionist in his technique and Symbolist as regards his content. The artist was very fond of this work, which as soon as he had painted it in 1896 was sent to exhibitions in Munich and Zurich. It belongs to the "mystical" series of his later years, yet it is also a successful return to the themes of peasant life and mountain landscapes which were so typical of his painting in the 1880s.

The enormous work entitled *Human Flood* by Giuseppe Pellizza da Volpedo (Volpedo, Alessandria, 1868-1907), donated in 1986, is a fitting close to the nineteenth century. The painting, which was executed between 1895 and 1897 and left unfinished, is the intermedi-

Giovanni Segantini, Spring Pastures.

ate version of the *Fourth Estate*, the monumental and ambitious work dedicated by the artist to the working-classes which was rapidly adopted by the socialists as a symbolic representation of the class struggle and the emancipation of the proletariat.

The Twentieth Century: The Jesi Collection
It is only recently that the art of the twentieth century has been incorporated in the collections of the Brera Gallery. This development is closely linked to those sensitive and far-sighted collectors and patrons such as Emilio and Maria Jesi and directors such as Franco Russoli and Carlo Bertelli who did all that was in their power to turn the Brera into a truly modern art gallery.

Until the late seventies the Brera possessed a few works by Birolli, Guttuso, Mafai, Marussig, Migneco and others purchased between 1939 and 1942 thanks to the Bergamo Prize, which unlike the Cremona Prize, which was tightly tied to the cultural policy of the Fascist regime, was prepared to recognise interests and merits of the contemporary Neo-Realist and Expressionist movements. Hence the

Self-portrait of 1908 by Umberto Boccioni (Reggio Calabria 1882-Verona 1916), donated in 1951 by the artist's friend and patron Vico Baer, was for years displayed together with the nineteenth century collection with the excuse that it was one of the last off-shoots of the Divisionist movement.

Since 1976, with the gift of fifty-six paintings and sculptures, followed in 1984 by another sixteen, on the part of Maria Jesi in accordance with the wishes of her husband Emilio, to whose memory it was dedicated, the Brera Gallery possesses a collection of modern art which for the coherence and the excellence of the works, some of which are very rare (for example the Metaphysical paintings of Morandi and Carrà) is unparalleled in the other state art galleries. Moreover, it includes some of the finest works produced by Italian artists from 1910 to 1940, with interesting specialisations (Morandi and De Pisis) and with some artists having an international flavour: Modigliani, Bonnard, Severini, Picasso, Braque, Estève and Wols.

The group of sculptures centres on three names: Medardo Rosso, the only nineteenth

century artist, Arturo Martini and Marino Marini. The three wax sculptures by Medardo Rosso (Turin 1858-Milan 1928), the Little *Laughing Girl* (1890), the *Jewish Child* (1892) and the *Veiled Woman* (1893), which for their effects of atmospheric fusion can be considered precursors of Futurist penetration of space (the interest in Rosso on the part of Boccioni, who referred to him in the *Technical Manifesto of Futurist Sculpture* is perhaps evidence of this), were executed in the years spent in Paris. Even if their roots were in the great Realist movement of the nineteenth century, with their changeable, evasive character they indicate that it had now been superseded.

Equally charming and rich in effects of light, but totally different as regards its nature and cultural affinities is the terracotta *Ophelia* or *Tomb of a Young Girl* of 1933 by Arturo Martini (Treviso 1889-Vado Ligure, near Savona 1947). He was the leading Italian sculptor of the first half of the twentieth century, who with uncommon versatility and sensibility was able to work in all the materials which are normally used for sculpture, including plaster, marble, terracotta, bronze, stone, wood and even ceramics, always managing to exploit their peculiarities with a suitable style which was never quite the same as before.

Archaism and Classicism were common ground for Martini and Marino Marini (Pistoia 1901-Viareggio 1980), a sculptor, painter and engraver who was linked to the Jesi by the special bond of friendship that sometimes forms between patron and artist. Thanks to these similarities the transition from smooth sculpture with, however, a large number of angularities like Martini's *The Drinker* (1926) to the *Nude of a Young Boy* of 1928 and *Pomona* of 1935 to the *Portrait of Emilio Jesi* can take place without it being overly traumatic.

The collection of paintings, which is much larger and more varied, begins with the brutally elegant, angular *Portrait of Moisè Kisling* and the *Portrait of a Young Girl*, which

is more obvious and routine. These works, which were both painted in 1915 by Amadeo Modigliani (Leghorn 1884-Paris 1920), were flanked by the *Portrait of a Man in a Hat* (1917) until it was stolen in 1986; this sequence confirmed the exceptional refinement, almost mannerist in intensity, and the artistic interests of Modigliani, which included Cézanne, Gauguin and his contemporaries Picasso and Brancusi, as well as African sculpture.

Futurism and Classicism, which were of crucial importance in the career of Gino Severini (Cortona, Tuscany 1883-Paris 1966)—who, like Modigliani, settled in Paris—are evident in the radiant *North-South Train* of 1912, with its Cubist affinities, and in *Still Life with a Pumpkin* of 1917, followed by *Still Life with a Fruit Bowl* of 1918, in which it is possible to perceive an interest in Classicism and Purism that has a parallel in the Synthetic Cubism in works by Picasso and Juan Gris.

In its turn the rebellious but optimistic consciousness of progress and the frenzied, deafening rhythm of modern life, which the Futurists proclaimed with noisily polemical speeches and unusual manifestos, may be appreciated in the study for the large, famous painting entitled *The City Rises* of 1910-11 and the equally famous *Riot in the Galleria* of 1911 by Umberto Boccioni. These works herald the themes and forms of the "plastic dynamism" which the artist was very soon to put into practice, illustrating it with lucidly expounded theories.

Wholly Futurist is the work by Carlo Carrà (Quargnento, near Alessandria in Piedmont 1881-Milan 1966) entitled *Rhythms of Objects* (1911), which is a measured and delicate marquetry of rotating forms. And so are *Watermelon and Liqueurs* by Ardengo Soffici (Rignano sull'Arno, near Florence 1879-Poggio a Caiano, also near Florence 1964) and *The Carpenter's Bench* by Ottone Rosai (Florence 1895-Ivrea, Piedmont 1957). Both of these works were painted in 1914 and they constitute a Tuscan variation on the Futurist credo, based on a looser and more casual rela-

Amadeo Modigliani, Portrait of Moisè Kisling.

106

tionship between objects, a return to primitivism and the use of bright colours. On the other hand, *The Lorry* and *The Studio of the Wonders* of 1917 by Mario Sironi (Sassari, Sardinia 1895-Milan 1961), with their monumental structure displaying architectural overtones are precursors of Metaphysical painting.

Between 1915 and 1918 or 1919 the magic and disturbing dream world of Metaphysical painting had its heyday, with its cult of the irrational, obscure symbols and parodies of the past. Giorgio de Chirico, who with his brother Andrea (Alberto Savinio) was the creator and prophet of the movement, is not present in the collection, even though the Jesi possessed works by the artist, but there are, however, works by Carrà, Morandi and, although he was less involved, Sironi.

Carrà in *Mother and Son, The Metaphysical Muse* and *The Enchanted Room*, painted in Ferrara in 1917 plagiarised his friend de Chirico, from whom he borrowed without any hesitation the bizarre props (mannequins, the flotsam and jetsam of mysterious attics, stage floors and long shadows), but he rejected his subtle irony, which he condemned as "a disrupting illness, discontent, the unconscious vengeance of the spirit," in order to seek, with a fluid style in which the enamel-like paint was applied in a number of layers, "our harmony in the things which surround us." Giorgio Morandi (Bologna 1890-1964) in his *Still Life* of 1918 and in the two of 1919, all of which are almost monochrome, gently austere and immersed in sublime calm, incorporated with serene equanimity only some of the features of Metaphysical aesthetics: the beauty of stillness, the taste for the classical and geometry and the sense of hesitating wonder—but nothing else.

The classical reaction, which was spreading in the Metaphysical movement and which was given a voice by Mario Broglio's periodical "*Valori Plastici*" (1919-22), metamorphosed in 1923 into the movement known as *Novecento*, a group of painters which was first met in Milan, growing out of all propor-

Carlo Carrà, The Metaphysical Muse.

Giorgio Morandi, Pink Landscape.
Filippo De Pisis, Sacred Fish.

tion almost until the outbreak of the Second World War and including an enormous variety of artists. The group's vague and conservative programme consisted in "proclaiming oneself Italian, traditionalists and modernists" had as a "unitary objective... clearly-delineated form, composure in the conception, nothing strange and nothing eccentric" and by celebrating "commonsense" it cleared the way for every possible eclecticism, at the same time provoking provincial narrow-mindedness. Thus it was the usual archaism and sense of isolation, which had already been experienced by the Metaphysical artists, which sustained the best works of the *Novecento* artists. This was true of *The Concertino* or the *Orchestra of the Paskowsky Café* and *Tuscan Street* of 1919 by Ottone Rosai, the three bleak *Urban Landscapes* painted between 1920 and 1923 by Mario Sironi, the famous, repulsive *House of Love* of 1922 by Carlo Carrà and the enchanted and thoroughly feminine *Garden* by Massimo Campigli (Florence 1895-St.Tropez 1971).

Altogether another matter was the *Scuola Romana*, which between 1928 and 1933 openly dissented with the *Novecento* movement and the official stance of the Fascist regime. It began to produce an instinctive style of painting, giving greater importance to emotions and spontaneity of vision guided by impulses which had Expressionist origins. Thus there were the gloomy, Neo-Baroque obsessions of *Cardinal Vannutelli on his Deathbed* by Scipione (Gino Bonichi) (Macerata, Marches 1904-Arco, near Trento 1933) or the *Carcass of an Ox* by Mario Mafai (Rome 1902-1965), both painted in 1930, the dull and messy appearance of the *Dry Flowers* of 1932, also by Mafai, and the *Archaeological Walk*, dangerously close to being naive, by Antonietta Raphael (Vilnius, Lithuania 1900-Rome 1975). Something of an exception in the Jesi collection are the series of paintings by Morandi and De Pisis, which may be consid-

ered perfect critical anthologies of the output of the two artists. Morandi was a refined painter with a contemplative nature, who was contrary to anything that was garish or excessively modern and who never left Bologna, where he worked alone but not in isolation, rigorously devoting himself to still lifes and the occasional landscape. In this atmosphere of perfect coherence and continuity, the result of unceasing, subtle meditation are the *Pink and Blue Flowers* of 1916, the *Still Life* of 1921, which is given a touch of drama with its altered colours, the other splendid and complex *Still Life with the Round Table* of 1929, the landscapes after Cézanne of 1914 and 1916 and the disarmingly simple ones of 1925, 1932 and 1936.

Filippo Tibertelli De Pisis (Ferrara 1896-Milan 1956), a poet and writer who started painting as an amateur, managed to create a heterodox style based on a unique calligraphic style, splendidly decorative and full of colour, capable of expressing the most varied and joyful visual impressions. While the *Still Life with Eggs* of 1924 and, above all, the *Sacred Fish* of 1925 are belated, overt homage to de Chirico, whom he had met in Ferrara in 1916 with Savinio and Carrà, the *Marine Still Life with Scampi* of 1926, the *Still Life with a Lapwing* of 1927 and the *Marine Still Life with a Feather* of 1953, the famous last work of the artist, continued to be Metaphysical from a conceptual point of view with the disconcerting juxtapositions and the unusual compositions that included vast skies, deserted beaches and solitary objects. The *Views of Paris*, the *San Moisè* of 1931 and the various still lifes with fruit baskets, peonies, flowers and bottles, flowers on window-sills, flowers in glasses and books painted between 1935 and 1945 are evidence of his overwhelming passion for the image and his capacity as an aesthete brimming over with vitality who was always ready to react to the stimuli offered by the surrounding world.

Select Bibliography

110

F. Algarotti, "Lettera pittorica sulla Romagna a P.-J. Mariette, 1761," in G. Bottari, S. Ticcozzi, *Lettere pittoriche...*, Milan 1822-23.

G. Bottari-S. Ticcozzi, *Raccolta di lettere sulla pittura, scultura ed architettura scritte dai più celebri personaggi dei secoli XV, XVI e XVII*, 8 vols., Milan, 1822-25: I, 1822; III, 1822.

J. Burckhardt, *Der Cicerone*, Basel 1855.

A. Caimi, *Delle arti del disegno nelle province di Lombardia dal 1777 al 1862*, Milan 1862.

F. Dall'Ongaro, *Scritti d'arte*, Milan 1873.

J. M. Friedlander, "La Galerie von Kaufmann à Berlin," in *L'art Flamand et Hollandais*, VI, 1906, pp. 39-40.

J. M. Friedlander, "Der Meister der Virgo inter Virgines," in *Jahrbuch der Preuzischen Kunstsammlungen*, XXXI, 1910, pp. 64-72.

W. Suida, *Leonardo und Sein Kreis*, Leipzig 1929.

Il catalogo della mostra del manierismo piemontese e lombardo del Seicento, edited by G. Testori, Turin-Ivrea 1955.

R. Longhi, *Officina Ferrarese*, Florence 1956.

Arte Lombarda dai Visconti agli Sforza, introduction by R. Longhi, Milan 1958.

Tanzio da Varallo, exhibition catalogue edited by G. Testori, Turin 1959.

A. Emiliani, *Il Bronzino*, Milan 1960.

C. Maltese, *Storia dell'arte italiana 1785-1943*, Turin 1960.

Il Morazzone, exhibition catalogue edited by M. Gregori, Varese 1962.

K. G. Boon, "De Meester van der Virgo inter Virgines," in *Oud Deft*, II, 1963, pp. 5-35.

G. A. Dell'Acqua, S. Matalon, *Affreschi lombardi del Trecento*, Milan 1963.

J. Pope-Hennessy, *Raffaello*, Italian translation, Turin 1963.

Il Cerano, exhibition catalogue edited by M. Rosci, Novara 1964.

G. A. Dell'Acqua, F. Mazzini, *Affreschi lombardi del Quattrocento*, Milan 1965.

C. Volpe, *La pittura riminese del Trecento*, Milan 1965.

A. Meli, "Pittura e pittori in Santa Maria Maggiore nella seconda metà del Trecento," in *Bergomum 1967*, nos. 3 and 4.

H. Gerson, *Rembrandt Gemälde*, Gütersloh 1968.

D. Posner, *Annibale Carracci*, London 1971.

Il Seicento lombardo, exhibition catalogue, Milan 1973.

C. Pirovano, *La pittura in Lombardia*, Milan 1973.

H. Brigstocke, "Giulio Cesare Procaccini Reconsidered," in *Jahrbuch der Berliner Museen*, 1976.

F. Franchini Guelfi, *Alessandro Magnasco*, Genoa 1977.

D. C. Ewing, *The Paintings and Drawings of Jan de Beer*, University of Michigan, Ann Arbor 1978.

S. J. Freedberg, *The Penguin History of Art, Painting in Italy 1500-1600*, Harmondsworth, Middlesex 1979.

N. W. Neilson, *Camillo Procaccini (circa 1555-1629), Paintings and Drawings*, London-New York 1979.

D. A. Brown, *The Young Correggio and His Leonardesque Sources*, New York-London 1981.

R. Pallucchini, *La pittura veneziana del Seicento*, Milan 1981.

K. Christiansen, *Gentile da Fabriano*, London 1982.

P. Fossati, "Pittura e Scultura fra le due guerre," in *Storia dell'Arte Italiana. Il Novecento*, Turin 1982.

M. Gregori, *Giacomo Ceruti*, Milan 1982.

Il Gotico a Siena, exhibition catalogue, Siena 1982.

M. M. Lamberti, "1870-1915. I mutamenti del mercato e le ricerche degli artisti," in *Storia dell'Arte italiana. Il Novecento*, Turin 1982.

S. Pinto, "La promozione delle arti negli Stati italiani," in *Storia dell'Arte Italiana. Il Settecento e l'Ottocento*, Turin 1982.

M. Cinotti, G. A. Dell'Acqua, *Michelangelo Merisi detto il Caravaggio*, Bergamo 1983.

Franceso Cairo 1607-1665, exhibition catalogue, Varese 1983.

Civiltà del Seicento a Napoli, exhibition catalogue, Naples 1984.

N. Bona Castellotti, *La Pittura Lombarda del '600*, Milan 1985.

A. Colombi Ferretti, *Girolamo Genga a Cesena*, Bologna 1985.

A. Emiliani, *Federico Barocci*, Bologna 1985.

M. Bona Castellotti, *La pittura lombarda del '700*, Milan 1986.

Il polittico di Andrea di Bartolo nella Pinacoteca di Brera, edited by V. Maderna, Florence 1986.

P. Zampetti, *Carlo Crivelli*, Florence 1986.

G. Algeri, "Pittura in Lombardia nel primo Quattrocento," in *La Pittura in Italia. Il Quattrocento*, Milan 1987, pp. 53-71 *et. seq.*

G. Ferri Piccaluga, "Ebrei nell'iconografia lombarda del Quattrocento," in *Rassegna mensile di Israel*, Vol. LII, nos. 2-3, 1987, pp. 357 *et. seq.*

P. C. Marani, *Leonardo e i leonardeschi a Brera*, Florence 1987.

M. Natale, "La Pittura in Lombardia nel secondo Quattrocento," in *La Pittura in Italia. Il Quattrocento*, Milan 1987, pp. 72-98.

Subleyras 1699-1749, exhibition catalogue, Rome 1987.

G. Algeri, F. Autelli, S. Bandera, M. T. Binaghi, G. Bora, M. T. Fiorio, P. C. Marani, F. Moro, M. Natale, C. Travi in *Pinacoteca di Brera. Scuole lombarda e piemontese 1300-1535*, edited by F. Zeri, Milan 1988.

Arte in Lombardia tra Gotico e Rinascimento, edited by M. Boskovitis, Milan 1988.

M. T. Fiorio, "Pittura in Lombardia nel Primo Cinquecento," in *La pittura in Italia. Il Cinquecento*, Milan 1988, pp. 49-76.

E. Larsen, *The Paintings of Anthony van Dyck*, Freren-Liège 1988.

H. Brigstocke, "Giulio Cesare Procaccini (1574-1625): ses attachés génoises et quelques autres faits nouveaux," in *Revue de l'art*, no. 85, 1989, pp. 45-60.

S. Coppa, *La pittura lombarda del '600 e del '700 nella Pinacoteca di Brera*, Florence 1989.

Il polittico di San Luca di Andrea Mantegna (1453-1545) in occasione del suo restauro, edited by S. Bandera Bistoletti, Florence 1989.

M. Jaffé, *Rubens. Catalogo completo*, Milan 1989.

La Pittura nel Veneto - Il Quattrocento, edited by Mauro Lucco, Milan 1989.

Pinacoteca di Brera. Scuole lombarda, ligure e piemontese, 1535-1700, edited by F. Zeri, Milan 1989.

Giovanni Gerolamo Savoldo fra Foppa, Giorgione e Caravaggio, exhibition catalogue, Milan 1990.

Il ritrovamento del Corpo di San Marco del Tintoretto: vicende e restauri, edited by R. Tardito, 1990.

Nuovi studi su Paolo Veronese, edited by M. Gelmin (Acts of the conference, Venice 1986), 1990.

A. Paolucci, *Piero della Francesca*, Florence 1990.

Pinacoteca di Brera. Scuola Veneta, edited by F. Zeri, Milan 1990.

Various Authors, *La Pittura in Italia: l'Ottocento*, edited by E. Castelnuovo, Milan 1990.

L. Galli, "Restauro e ritrovamento: novità sugli affreschi dell'Oratorio di Mocchirolo," in *Arte Cristiana*, no. 745, 1991, pp. 310-312.

Giovanni Ambrogio di Predis 1455-1508
Ambrogio da Fossano 1450-1522
detto il Bergognone
Carlo Crivelli 1435-1493

940   Best Canaletto ever seen

Photographic Credits
Electa Archives, Milan;
Scala, Florence.

Printed for Electa by
Fantonigrafica - Elemond Editori Associati